Linux Command-Line Tips & Tricks

Terrific Techniques To Take The Tedium Off Terminal Tasks

V. Subhash

Linux Command-Line Tips & Tricks

Written, designed & produced
(using only *free and open-source software*) **by**
V. Subhash
www.VSubhash.in

Copyright

Edition

Second edition published in 2022. (First edition published in 2021.) This second-edition paperback is probably **the first and only printed book to have syntax-highlighted code in full colour**.

ISBN

9789357683043 (for 2nd edition)

List Of Contents

- **Chapters**

  - **Terminal** [6]
    ☆ Your terminal program ☆ Use the `~/.bashrc` file ☆ Create command aliases ☆ Start at the desktop ☆ Terminal font ☆ Terminal colours ☆ Use `bash`, not `sh` ☆ BASH history ☆ Forget this command ☆ Break-up long commands ☆ Return to your previous directory ☆ Return to your home directory ☆ Use pushd and popd ☆ Switch to a TTY Terminal ☆ Do not use elevated file manager for elevated everything ☆ BASH shortcuts ☆ History expansion character (!) ☆ Browse recent commands ☆ Regular expressions ☆ Persistent environment variables

  - **Shell Scripting** [14]
    ☆ Write shell scripts ☆ Conditional operators ☆ String comparison ☆ For loops ☆ Breaking out of nested loops ☆ For your for loops ☆ Limited-scope variables ☆ Reading text input ☆ Reading lines of a text file efficiently ☆ Shell script variables ☆ Beware of $? ☆ Basename, file name and extension ☆ Command substitution (backtick alternative) ☆ Arrays ☆ Variable substitution ☆ Arithmetic operations ☆ `awk` ☆ Regular expressions in `sed` ☆ Library of functions or include files ☆ Protect your scripts ☆ Where art thou /dev/null? ☆ Use `printf` instead of `echo` ☆ Display notifications ☆ Delay a task ☆ Here document ☆ Use a GUI widget for elevated privileges ☆ Use GUI widgets for prompts ☆ Cut from the middle ☆ Beware of undefined variables ☆ Handle errors or stop execution ☆ Escaping ☆ Printer's error ☆ Your own secret scripting mimetype

  - **Caja Actions Configuration** [32]
    ☆ Copy filename ☆ Copy pathname ☆ Rename a file with the datestamp ☆ Silence a video ☆ Encrypt a PDF with a password

  - **System Administration** [37]
    ☆ List only directories ☆ Schedule tasks ☆ Run tasks after a delay ☆ Move files to the Trash ☆ Delete files forever ☆ Find the full path of a file ☆ Hard vs. soft links ☆ Recursively delete files or directories ☆ System Cleanup ☆ Run as `root` ☆ Run in the background ☆ Run in the background without getting killed ☆ Startup programs ☆ Run as another user ☆ Force update with Internet time servers ☆ Change GRUB2 wallpaper ☆ Restore GRUB using chroot jail ☆ Adjust screen brightness ☆ Disable touchpad ☆ Reassign mouse button functions ☆ Disable radio devices ☆ Disable webcam ☆ Detect IP of a LAN node ☆ Use a RAM drive ☆ Manage `tar` and `gz` files ☆ `apt`, `aptitude` or `apt-get` ☆ Build from source ☆ Convert text files off the Internet ☆ Wine prefixes ☆ Use `telnet` and `nslookup` to test email servers

- o **Internet Tasks** [51]

  ☆ Download a file no matter what   ☆ Download online videos   ☆ Use multiple Firefox profiles   ☆ Modify `about:config` settings in Firefox   ☆ Make Seamonkey Mail display dates properly   ☆ Ad-blocker hosts file   ☆ Use NetCheck   ☆ Check for valid links   ☆ More `wget` tips   ☆ Automate FTP tasks   ☆ Check media hype with `curl`   ☆ Do whois lookups

- o **Multimedia Tasks** [61]

  ☆ Run custom commands with image viewers   ☆ Extract GIF frames   ☆ Convert transparent PNGs to JPEGs with white background   ☆ MIDI in Linux   ☆ ASCII art from images   ☆ Disable laptop speaker and enable headphone output   ☆ Run Audacious like Winamp   ☆ FFmpeg

- o **Office Tasks** [73]

  ☆ Use a text browser   ☆ Calender   ☆ Use MarkDown for text documents   ☆ Convert text to HTML with Unicode encoding   ☆ Convert HTML to ODT, DOCX and PDF   ☆ Convert HTML to MarkDown   ☆ Convert PDF to images   ☆ Convert images to PDF   ☆ Print to PDF   ☆ Combine PDFs   ☆ Decrypt PDF   ☆ Convert PDF to DjVu   ☆ Check pixel density (DPI) of an image   ☆ Set pixel density of an image   ☆ Check for embedded colour profiles in an image   ☆ Save image with CMYK colour profile   ☆ Remove embedded colour profile in an image   ☆ Set image quality   ☆ Grab a screenshot of a web page

- o **Miscellaneous Tips & Tricks** [81]

  ☆ Compose key   ☆ Typing by Unicode value   ☆ Rupee symbol   ☆ Type Unicode flag symbols   ☆ Launch a file in its default GUI application   ☆ Move processes to a different core   ☆ Use Seamonkey   ☆ GreaseMonkey scripts   ☆ Disable Javascript   ☆ Use Stylus   ☆ Select text inside a link   ☆ Caja tips

- **Books by V. Subhash**

- **About the author**

Introduction

I think I was destined to write this book because my name is made of two very important shell commands - `su` (superuser) and `bash` (shell). I have been using Linux for twenty years now but it was only 12 years ago that I made a full switch. By then, most of the hardware driver issues had been sorted out. In fact, Linux did better with new hardware. I had a WCDMA USB modem and it routinely crashed my Windows computer. On Ubuntu, I used a `wvdial` script and the modem became faster! Not once did the Linux OS crash.

I liked the way how Linux could be configured with just text scripts. With Windows, your options became zero if the manufacturer did not provide a compatible driver. I had worked on a Unix system (SCO) 25 years ago and was quite proficient with shell scripting. This new OS seemed like something I had always wanted - endless tinkering.

Although I found the Gnome 2 as a perfectly designed desktop, I used dozens of shell scripts to automate things and save time. (I despised Gnome 3 and was happy when the Mate Desktop project continued the Gnome 2 legacy.) The shell, by then, was not just the `sh`. It was now `bash`, a more evolved and sophisticated version. I did not know that there was a difference. The `sh` in my system was like the old Unix shell. Several of the shell programming constructs that I found online did not work with it. It was really a forehead-slapping moment when I learned that I had to start all shell scripts with `bash` rather than `sh`. What a world of difference this change brought!

Later, I read somewhere (probably Slashdot) that O'Reilly or somebody had made the book *SAMS Teach Yourself Shell Programming In 24 Hours* free. I refer to its PDF almost every week - usually for the same things. (I can program in more than a dozen languages and I can remember nothing for sure.) While this SAMS book was fantastic, there is some information that you can only find in an another book - the *BASH Reference Manual* published by the *Free Software Foundation*. (This book has no examples. It is like a briefing document useful only for those who will be working with the source code.) I needed a ready reference that would replace these two books. Not entirely... just the stuff I need oftentimes. After I wrote *FFmpeg Quick Hacks* book, I do not search online forums for answers to my FFmpeg problems. My book has all the answers... almost all. 😬 I expect this book to do just as well for BASH.

This book is at an advanced level. It assumes that you already know how to use the terminal and `bash`. It does not teach you the basics or try to be a comprehensive reference. It trusts your intuition and focuses on things you are most likely to forget. For example, it does not mention that pressing Ctrl+e will take you to the end of the line. You already know that pressing the END key has the same effect. Traditionalist to the core, I have followed the minimalistic approach of the BASH manual but have avoided the cryptic descriptions. I expect you to quickly understand whatever I have written.

V. Subhash

Kerala, INDIA
www.VSubhash.in

Terminal

- **Your terminal program:** My terminal of choice is *Terminator*. In addition to tabs, Terminator supports split windows (vertically and horizontally). You can display a man page (help) in one and execute the examples in another.

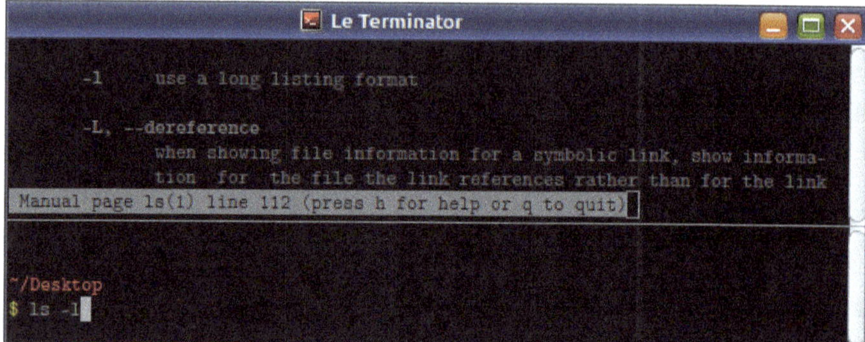

- **Use the `~/.bashrc` file:** Commands in the hidden `.bashrc` file are executed before the terminal window is displayed. Several terminal settings are stored in this file. You can make changes to it using a text editor. When you change a setting, copy the original lines and comment them (place a '#' sign before each line).

- **Create command aliases:** You can create abbreviated forms for your commands in the `.bashrc` file. If you have an alias like this in your `.bashrc` file, you can type the letter l instead of the command 'ls -l'.

```
alias l='ls -l'
```

To execute my 'kill script' [14], I use another alias:

```
alias kll='bash ~/MyScripts/killit.txt '
```

So, to kill Firefox, I type 'kll firefox'.

- **Start at the desktop:** While you could put a 'cd' command in your `.bashrc` file, a better option is to use '--working-directory' parameter of the terminal command of your launcher. This ensures that new tabs open in the last working directory rather than the desktop.

```
mate-terminal --working-directory=/home/ya-username/Desktop
```

- **Terminal font:** If you are spending considerable time on the terminal, it is important to use a good font for it. The ancient *CMU Typewriter Text* font (by Donald Knuth) looks bad on most modern GUI applications but is unsurpassed on the terminal.

  If you do not have privileges to install fonts, then you can copy this or any other font to your `~/.local/fonts` directory. After adding/removing fonts, you need to run this command:

```
fc-cache -rf
```

- **Terminal colours:** Some terminals have a white background. Change its background to black and foreground to green. It is easy on the eye and more readable. When you want to quickly find information or if you spend a lot of time looking at the terminal, you do not want to suffer a big wall of white.

White-on-black or green-on-black colour schemes are fine but why limit yourself? Linux offers much more than two colours. Open the `.bashrc` file and add this line at the end.

```
PS1="\a\n\n\[\e[31;1m\]\u@\h on \d at \@\n\[\e[33;1m\]\w\
[\e[0m\]\n\[\e[32;1m\]\$ \[\e[0m\]"
```

This will show you the current time, date and directory on the prompt while reserving almost the entire width of the terminal for your epic shell commands.

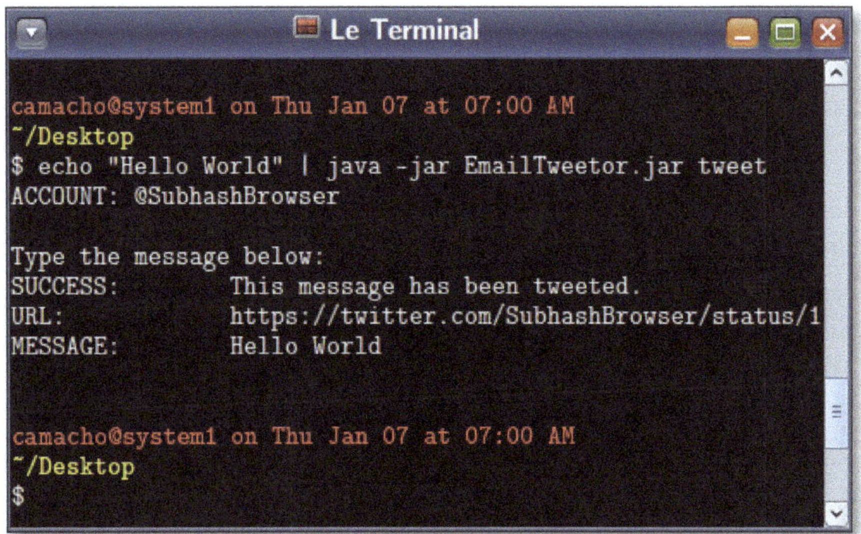

If that is information overload, then you could use a minimal style:

```
PS1="\a\n\n\[\e[31;1m\]\w\n\[\e[33;1m\]\$ \[\e[0m\]"
```

You can craft your own prompt variable using codes mentioned in the *IBM Developer Works* Linux library article *'Prompt Magic'*. However, here are the basic rules:

○ The prompt variable can have the following codes:

Code	Effect	Code	Effect
\n	New line	\t	Tab
\u	Username	\$	$ or # (root)
\w	Current directory path	\W	Current directory name

\h	Hostname	\H	Full hostname
\a	ASCII bell	\\	Backslash
\t	24-hour time	\T	12-hour time
\@	12-hour time with am/pm	\d	Date
\u	Username	\w	Current directory

- o Codes that do not take up space, such as colour codes, need to begin with `\[` and end with `\]`.
- o Colour codes need to begin with `\e[` and end in `m`. Foreground and background colours have to be separated by a semi-colon(;). Adding `;1m` makes a colour bolder. At the end, add `\e[0m` to reset your Rembrandt back to normal.

Foreground	Background	Number
30	40	Black/Gray
31	41	Red
32	42	Green
33	43	Yellow
34	44	Blue
35	45	Purple
36	46	Cyan
37	47	White

- **Use bash, not sh:** My first experience with a Unix-like OS was on SCO Unix. As a result, I was accustomed to running shell script files with sh command. This continued even after I started using GNU/Linux systems. For years, I was perplexed why many of the scripts were not working well. Apparently, in many GNU/Linux distributions, sh refers to the old Unix-like shell and bash is a separate program and works like a more advanced superset of sh. As a result, scripts designed for bash (Bourne Again shell) will not work well with sh (Bourne shell). So, always use bash to run all your bash shell scripts. However, there are some tasks, such as the proprietary nVidia graphics driver compilation, that still requires sh. Another thing to note is that the *su* or *root* terminal uses sh by default. This is why the Up/Down arrow keys will not let you browse the history. So, be aware of which shell program you are currently using.
- **BASH history:** The commands you type in the bash prompt is stored in a file named .bash_history in your home directory. While you can browse the bash history using the Up and Down arrow keys at the prompt, you can also do a search on the history using the keyboard shortcut "Ctrl+R". (You can abandon it by pressing Ctrl+G.) You can increase the length of the command history by changing the following variables in the .bashrc file. They limit the number of lines of typed commands that can be stored in memory and in the .bash_history file.

```
HISTSIZE=2000
HISTFILESIZE=20000
```

- **Forget this command:** If you do not want the bash history to record a command, begin it with a space.

- **Return to your previous directory:** Just type `cd -` to return to your last working directory.
- **Return to your home directory:** The `cd` command without any parameters returns to your `$HOME` directory.
- **Use `pushd` and `popd`:** If you `cd` everywhere, you will have to carefully remember and type the path. Instead, make `pushd` remember your current working directory and make `popd` return to it.

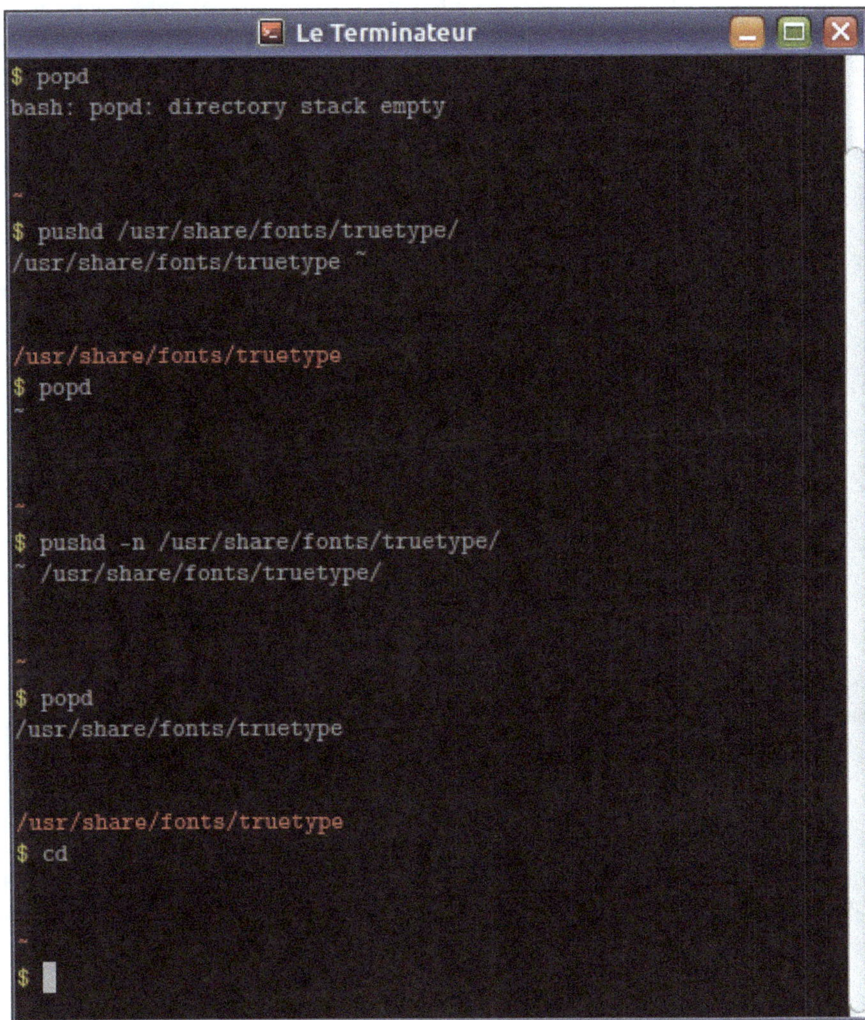

- **Break up long commands:** When you have to type a long command, you can type a "slash" to continue the command on the next line. Do not leave any space characters after the slash.

```
ffmpeg -i tank.mp4 \
       -c:v copy    \
       -c:a copy    \
```

```
    -ss 1:12     \
    -t  2:50     \
    tank-cut.mp4
```

- **Switch to a TTY Terminal:** The Linux desktop managers are known to be very stable. However, in the rare occurrence when the desktop hangs, you can hold down "Ctrl+Alt" and press any of the function keys to switch to a "TTY terminal". These terminals are created by the OS before loading the GUI (desktop manager). From one of these terminals, you can login to your account and do your troubleshooting. Sometimes, some programs (new websites on old Firefox) can lock up the desktop. The only option is to go to a TTY terminal and kill the offending program. In the rare occasions that the desktop manager locks up, you can try one of the following:

```
sudo service gdm restart
sudo service mdm restart
sudo service lightdm restart
sudo service gdm3 restart
```

- **Do not use elevated file manager for *elevated everything*:** If you launch Nautilus or Caja (the file manager) with elevated privileges, any file click will result in launching the file-type-handler application with elevated privileges. This application may not be designed to run like that. Mistakes can be catastrophic. It will also mess up file permissions and user/group ownerships.

- **BASH shortcuts:** Traditional keyboard shortcuts for copy and paste do not work in the terminal. You need to use Ctrl+Shift+c and Ctrl+Shift+v for the same.

Ctrl + C	Discard the currently typed command
Ctrl + L	Clear screen (same as `clear`)
Ctrl + K	Delete everything after current cursor location
Alt + D	Delete the word after current cursor location
Ctrl + U	Cut everything before current cursor location
Ctrl + W	Cut the word previous to current cursor location
Ctrl + Y	Paste what you cut last
Ctrl + S	Stop screen output but not the command
Ctrl + Q	Resume screen output
Ctrl + Z	Move a long-running command to the background Use `bg`, `fg` and `wait` commands to access and control them.
Ctrl + X + X	Move cursor to the beginning of the command or return to previous cursor location
Ctrl + R	Search previous bash history
Ctrl + S	Search subsequent bash history
Alt + R	Discard your edits and restore the command selected from bash history
Ctrl + G	Abandon bash history search
!n	Execute nth command in bash history

!!	Execute last command (Equivalent to `!-1`)
Alt + .	Insert last word from the previous command (usually used after `mkdir` or `cat`)
!leword	Execute last command beginning with 'leword'
!?leword	Execute last command containing 'leword'
!?leword?whatever	Suffix 'whatever' to last command containing 'leword' and execute it
!^leword^whatever^	Replace 'whatever' in last command containing 'leword' and execute it

- **History expansion character (!)**: This is used to access commands stored in `bash` history file.

!n	Execute nth command in bash history
!!	Execute last command (Equivalent to `!-1`)
!leword	Execute last command *beginning* with 'leword'
!?leword?	Execute last command *containing* 'leword'
^search^replace	Execute last command after replacing first occurrence of 'search' with 'replace'

You can modify the history search using certain *word designators*, preceded by a colon (:).

!?leword?:0	Execute with 0th word (usually the command) in last command containing 'leword'
!?leword?:2	Execute with second word of last command containing 'leword'
!?leword?:$	Execute with last word in last command containing 'leword'
!?leword?:2-6	Execute with second word to sixth word in last command containing 'leword'
!?leword?:-6	Execute with all words up to 6th word in last command containing 'leword' (Equivalent to `!?leword?:0-6`)
!?leword?:*	Execute with all words of last command (but not the 0th word) containing 'leword' (Equivalent to `!?leword?:1-$`)
!?leword?:2*	Execute with the second word to the last word in last command (but not the 0th word) containing 'leword' (Equivalent to `!?leword?:2-$`)
!?leword?:2-	Execute with all words from the 2nd position to last but-one word and not the 0th word in the command containing 'leword'

☞ bash will execute whatever you have retrieved from the history with whatever you have already typed at the prompt.

You can also use any number *modifiers*, each preceded by a colon (:).

!?leword?**:p**	Display (but not execute) last command containing 'leword'
!?leword?**:t**	Execute with last command containing 'leword' after removing all pathname of last argument (i.e., leave the tail containing the file name)
!?leword?**:r**	Execute with last command containing 'leword' after removing the file extension from the last argument
!?leword?**:e**	Execute with last command containing 'leword' after removing pathname and file name from the last argument (leaving just the extension)
!?leword?**:s/search/replace**	Execute last command containing 'leword' after replacing the first instance of 'search' with 'replace'
!?leword?**:as**/search/replace	Execute last command containing 'leword' after replacing all instances of 'search' with 'replace'

☞ If you omit the search text ('leword') and use the *history expansion character* with the word designators and the modifiers, bash will search the last command.

☞ Until you become proficient in using the *history expansion character*, use the modifier :p to display the command before you actually execute it.

- **Browse recent commands**: The tac command is the opposite of the cat command. It can be used thusly.

```
tac ~/.bash_history | less
```

[I am sorry. I promise I will never use that phrase again.]

- **Regular Expressions** For several years, I had on my desk photocopies of a chapter from an MSDN CHM help file about regular expressions. I would often refer to them for this table. A *regular expression* uses text patterns composed of literal text strings and some special *metacharacters*.

\	Used to escape certain special characters
^	Matches the beginning of a line
$	Matches the end of a line
\A	Matches the beginning of a text string
\Z	Matches the end of a text string
\b	Matches a word boundary
\B	Matches anywhere except a word boundary
\<	Matches the beginning of a word
\>	Matches the end of a word
*	Matches the preceding character or expression zero or more times
+	Matches the preceding character or expression one or more

	times
?	Matches the preceding character or expression never or just once
{n}	Matches the preceding character or expression exactly n times
{n,}	Matches the preceding character or expression n or more times
{n,m}	Matches the preceding character or expression n to m times
?	When following a quantifier (such as `*,+,?,{n}`), it matches as few characters as possible
.	Matches any character except newline (\n)
x|y	Matches literals x or y
[xyz]	Matches a character in the enclosed character set
[^xyz]	Matches a character not in the enclosed character set
[a-z]	Matches a character in the enclosed character range.
[^a-z]	Matches a character not in the enclosed character range
(pattern)	Matches the pattern
(?:pattern)	Matches text followed by *pattern* (useful with x|y parts)
(?=pattern)	Matches text followed by *pattern* (useful with x|y parts)
(?!pattern)	Matches text not followed by *pattern* (useful with x|y parts)
\d	Matches a numeric digit (0-9)
\D	Matches a character that is not a numeric digit `[^0-9]`
\w	Matches an alphanumeric character or underscore `[a-z0-9_]`
\W	Matches a character that is not an alphanumeric character or underscore `[^a-z0-9_]`
\s	Matches any white-space character `[\n\r\f\t\v]`
\S	Matches any character that is not a white space `[^\n\r\f\t\v]`
\t	Matches a tab
\n	Matches the newline character
\r	Matches the carriage-return character
\num	Matches positive integer num
\uNNNN	Matches a Unicode codepoint as a four-digit hexadecimal number NNNN
\cx	Matches control character x

☞ Bash has its own similarly named '*patterns*' [14] so be mindful of the difference.

- **Persistent environment variables**: If you want certain variables to pre-exist anytime you open the terminal, then you can place them in the `.bashrc` file. However, scripts invoked from by desktop menu/launchers will not process the `.bashrc` file. You could instead declare them as global variables in the `/etc/environment` file.

Shell Scripting

- **Write shell scripts:** bash is not only an interactive command prompt, it is also a powerful scripting language interpreter. As many terminal tasks require more than one shell command, you can store them in a shell script text file and pass the variable data as command-line arguments.

  The following is my 'kill' script. You can set the first line of a script to `#!/bin/bash` and it will most likely be interpreted with bash even if it is launched with `sh`.

```bash
#!/bin/bash

for sID in $(pgrep -if $1)
do
  ps $sID
  if [ $sID -ne $$ ]; then
    kill -STOP $sID
    sleep 2
    kill -KILL $sID
  #else
    #echo No one moydured
  fi
done
```

  The `-f` switch of pgrep ensures that the match is made to the program arguments as well, not just the process name. Some of my background processes are Java apps that I wrote. Their process names are always 'java' because their JAR executables are always launched with the command `java -jar`. They get caught only when I use the `-f` switch.

  ☞ Some people do not use hashbang `#!/bin/bash` interpreter directive. To maintain portability with *unices* such as OpenBSD or FreeBSD, where bash does not exist in the `/bin` directory, they use `#!/usr/bin/env bash` expecting to env to find and run bash correctly. These *unices* are typically used in small-footprint devices such as firewalls, gateways, modem or NAS. If you are not expecting to make a transition to such a device, you better stick with `#!/bin/bash`.

- **Patterns**: These characters can be used to match text strings and filenames. You can create a *pattern list* using a pipe (|) as the delimiter with brackets. You can quote what looks like a pattern to force bash to treat it literally.

Pattern	Matches
*	All files in current directory
**	All files and directories in current directory
**/	All directories and their immediate (first-level) subdirectories The directory names will be suffixed by a backslash (/).
?	One character
[]	Any characters or range of characters (separated by a hyphen)

specified between the square brackets

If the first character is ! or ^, then characters not matching the specified characters are matched

The hyphen can be matched by specifying it last inside the brackets. The] character can be matched by specifying it first.

?( )	Zero or one occurrence of the pattern list.
*( )	Zero or more occurrences of the pattern list.
+( )	One or more occurrences of the pattern list.
@( )	One of the patterns in the list.
!( )	None of the patterns in the list.

- **Conditional operators:** I am unable to memorize these expression operators used with the `if` statement.

Operator use	Result
`[ -f "$file" ]`	Does it exist as a file?
`[ -d "$file" ]`	Does it exist as a directory?
`[ -h "$file" ]`	Does it exist as a soft link?
`[ -r "$file" ]`	Is the file readable?
`[ -w "$file" ]`	Is the file writeable?
`[ -x "$file" ]`	Is the file executable?
`[ -z "$string" ]`	Is the string empty?
`[ -n "$string" ]`	Is the string not empty?
`[ "$string1" = "$string2" ]`	Are the strings same? = is same as ==
`[ "$string1" != "$string2" ]`	Are the strings different?
`[ "$string1" < "$string2" ]`	Does first string sort ahead of second?
`[ "$string1" > "$string2" ]`	Does first string sort after second?
`[ n1 -eq n2 ]`	Are the numbers same?
`[ n1 -ne n2 ]`	Are the numbers different?
`[ n1 -le n2 ]`	Is n1 less than or equal to n2?
`[ n1 -ge n2 ]`	Is n1 greater than or equal to n2?
`[ n1 -lt n2 ]`	Is n1 less than n2?
`[ n1 -gt n2 ]`	Is n1 greater than n2?
`[ ! e ]`	Is the expression false
`[ e1 ] && [ e2 ]`	Are both expressions true?
`[ e1 ] || [ e2 ]`	Is one of the expressions true?

☞ Wonder what the double ampersands do in those daisy-chained commands you find on the Internet? It means that execute the first command and only when it finishes without error execute the second command.

```
mkdir foo && cd foo
```

☞ With the || operator, bash will evaluate (or execute) the second expression only if the first expression turns out to be false.

☞ Do not use -a and -o logical operators. You will make mistakes reading and writing them. They are the sh way of doing things. Square brackets are so bash.

☞ Ever wonder what is with the double square brackets, as in if [[$foo = "bar"]]? Apparently, the [is a program (/bin/[). The double squares behave like a keyword in bash. The expression between the double brackets is evaluated more literally. Strings are not split into words and file pathnames are not expanded. Other forms of expression expansion are performed. Operators such as =, ==, != have different meanings. There is support for a new =~ operator, which is not available in single-bracket evaluations.

Operator use	Result
`[[ string1 = string2 ]]`	Are the strings same?
	Behaves like == in single-square-bracket evaluations.
`[[ string1 == string2 ]]`	Does string1 match the pattern [14] string2?
`[[ string1 != string2 ]]`	Does string1 not match the pattern string2?
`[[ string1 =~ string2 ]]` (That's a tilde after the =)	Does string1 match the regular expression [12] string2?

The strings on the right side of ==, != and == can be quoted if they have to be treated as ordinary strings.

All of these operators return 0 if the evaluation is true and 1 if the evaluation is false. The =~ operator returns 2 if the regular expression has a syntax error.

Wonder why the expressions result in numbers instead of boolean values? That is how Unices work. (What? Linux is not a unix? Please!) When a program exits successfully, it exits with a return value of 0. If it exits with an error, it will return a non-zero value. Each value may be assigned for a different type of error. If you use true or false in test expressions, you are again dealing with command-line programs, usually stored as /usr/bin/true and /usr/bin/false. They are not keywords in the bash language.

The =~ operator is great for matching substrings.

```
# Matches substring ell
$ if [[ "Hello?" =~ ell ]]; then echo "Yes"; else echo "No"; fi
Yes
```

```
# Matches substring Hell at beginning
$ if [[ "Hello?" =~ ^Hell ]]; then echo "Yes"; else echo "No"; fi
Yes
```

```bash
# Does not match substring ? (a regex special character) at the
end
$ if [[ "Hello?" =~ ?$ ]]; then echo "Yes"; else echo "No"; fi
No


# Matches substring ? at the end when quoted
$ if [[ "Hello?" =~ "?"$ ]]; then echo "Yes"; else echo "No"; fi
Yes
```

Evaluations with double square brackets have their use-cases but they are not for all situations. You are comparing with text patterns, not ordinary text strings. The operators have slightly different meanings. There is a new operator and a new exit code. There are misleading advisories online that using double-square-brackets is the failsafe or the correct way to do evaluations. (Among them, I found one by Google developers. As the author of the public-domain *AndroidWithoutStupid* library, I am not surprised.)

- **String comparison:** When you set a string to a variable, there should be no space on either side of the assignment (=) operator. When you compare two strings, there should be a space on either side of the comparison (=) operator.

```bash
# Causes an error because 'sTest' looks like a command
# and '=' and '"hello"' become its arguments
sTest = "hello"


# Assigns string variable correctly
sTest="hello"


# Temporary assignment evaluates to true whatever the value
if [ "$sTest"="helloooooooooo" ]; then
    echo "Yep"
else
    echo "Nope"
fi


# String comparison evaluates to true
if [ "$sTest" = "hello" ]; then
    echo "Yep"
else
    echo "Nope"
fi
```

These mistakes are easy to make and the script will seem to run without any problem. However, they introduce serious logical errors.

- **For loops:** Iterating through files in the local directory is easy.

```bash
for sFile in *.jpg
```

```
do
  echo $sFile
done
```

- **For your for loops:** Every time you change the value of a variable, an angel dies or accelerates Global Warming... or Global Cooling, whichever you prefer. Use the `seq` command wherever you can.

- **Breaking out of nested loops:** By default, the `break` statement breaks out of the current loop. The `break` keyword also accepts a number parameter that makes it to break a specified number of levels outwards. For example, `break 2` would make the script to break two loops from where the break statement was encountered.
- **Limited-scope variables**: When you assign a value to a variable and then specify a command after that, the variable holds that value only for the sub-process of the shell in which the command is executing.

```
http_proxy='http://123.123.123.123:8080' wget -q -e use_proxy=yes
--spider --timeout=4 --tries=1 http://www.example.com
```

This is two commands in one. The first one sets a foreign proxy server to a variable. The second tests the proxy server using `wget`. Usually, `wget` will use the default proxy server of your network connection. By setting the variable `http_proxy`, you can force `wget` to use an alternate proxy specified by the variable. By placing the variable assignment before the command, you can limit the scope of the variable `http_proxy` only to the execution of the `wget` command. This is how you pass limited-scope variables to commands and scripts.

- **Reading input:** One command to read user input is `read`. For example:

```
read -p "Type Yes or No: " sChoice
if [ -z "$sChoice" ]; then
  echo "Assuming default No."
  exit
fi
```

Whatever is typed will be placed in the $sChoice variable. If the user did not type anything and just pressed the Enter key, then $sChoice will be empty. You can check that using [-z $sChoice] evaluation.

- **Reading lines of a text file efficiently** : By default, the `read` command splits the input line into words and assigns them to variables specified as its parameters. If there are more words than variables, then the last variable will be set with all the remaining words. It splits the input line using the $IFS environment variable (*Input Field Separator*) as the delimiter. This is usually a space character but not always. To make the read command efficient when it is reading a text file, set the delimiter to an empty string (IFS=). Then, it will read the entire line and and use only one variable. Then, it will quickly read each line as a whole and assign it to that variable.

```
while IFS= read -r sLine ; do
    echo "Read » ${sLine} «"


    # Rest of the line-processing code
done < some-text-file.txt
```

- **Shell script variables:** When bash executes a script, it creates these special parameters for the script.

Shell variable	Use
$0	Name of the shell script
$1, $2,...	Positional parameters or arguments passed to the script
$#	Total count of arguments passed to the script
$?	Exit status of last command
$*	All arguments (double-quoted)
$@	All arguments (individually double-quoted)
$$	Process ID of current shell/script
$_	Last argument of the previous command
$!	Process ID of last background process

At the terminal, $0 will usually expand to the shell program (/bin/bash). You can use the set command to specify parameters to the current shell *ipso facto*.

```
# Displays 0
echo $#


# Displays an empty string and causes a new line
echo $*


# Sets hello and world as parameters to current shell
set -- hello world


# Displays 2 (the number of parameters)
echo $#


# Displays world
echo $2


# Remove parameters to current shell
```

```bash
set --

# Displays 0 (as earlier)
echo $#
```

☞ The option `--` represents the end of options and implies that whatever following it must be command parameters.

- **Beware of** $?: The exit code (`$?`) changes with each statement. It can also change more than once within in one statement. In other words, `$?` can only be accessed once, as that access is another statement which has its own exit code and changes the `$?` variable. For example, this `if` statement will never echo "Failure or success".

  ```bash
  echo "Hello"

  if [ $? -eq 1 ] || [ $? -eq 0 ]; then
    echo "Failure or success"
  else
    echo "Something else"
  fi
  ```

  After the `echo` statement, $? becomes 0 (for success). The first evaluation of the `if` statement changes it to 1 (for failure). This means that second evaluation of the `if` statement will also result in failure. The correct way to do to this is to assign the exit code to a variable and then evaluate that variable.

  ```bash
  echo "Hello"

  iEC=$?

  if [ $iEC -eq 1 ] || [ $iEC -eq 0 ]; then
    echo "Failure or success"
  else
    echo "Something else"
  fi
  ```

- **Basename, file name and extension:** The last two commands will not remove the path if it is present. Use `basename` to remove the path of the file.

  ```bash
  # Outputs 'animalia-page-01.jpg'
  basename ~/Desktop/animalia-page-01.jpg


  # Stores output of the first command in a variable
  sFile=`basename ~/Desktop/animalia-page-01.jpg`


  # Outputs filename `animalia-page-01`
  echo ${sFile%.*}


  # Outputs extension `jpg`
  ```

```bash
echo ${sFile##*.}
```

- **Command substitution (backtick alternative):** If you want to use the output of another command in a line, you can place them within backquotes (`` `command command-arguments` ``). Reading or escaping this can get complicated when the command arguments also have quotation marks. For ease of use and clarity, you can place the command in a pair of brackets — `$(command)`.

- **Arrays:** Does every language out there need to have a totally different method to create arrays? Who so evil? Why?

```bash
# Creates an array
var=(hello world how are you)


# Displays hello
echo $var


# Displays how
echo ${var[2]}


# Changes hello to howdy
var[0]=howdy


# Displays howdy
echo ${var[0]}


# Displays values — howdy world how are you
echo ${var[@]}


# Displays values — howdy world how are you
echo ${var[*]}


# Displays indexes or keys — 0 1 2 3 4
echo ${!var[@]}


# Displays indexes or keys — 0 1 2 3 4
echo ${!var[*]}
```

```bash
# Displays dy
echo ${var:3:2}


# Displays rld
echo ${var[1]:2:3}


# Displays 5, the number of variables in the array
echo ${#var}
```

- **Variable substitution:** Because we need to be confused.

Substitution	Effect
${var1:-var2}	If `var1` is null or does not exist, `var2` is used
${var1:=var2}	If `var1` is null or does not exist, value of `var2` is used and set to `var1`
${var1:?msg}	If `var1` is null or does not exist, `msg` is displayed as error
${var1:+var2}	If `var1` exists, `var2` is used but not set to `var1`
${var:offset}	Everything of `var` after `offset` number of characters
	If @ or * is used in place of `var`, then it evaluates to arguments to the script starting from `offset` position.
${var:offset:length}	`length` number of characters of `var` after `offset` number of characters A negative offset starts from the end and grabs characters to the left. A negative length is interpreted in terms of offset, not length. Use space before minus.
	If @ or * is used in place of `var`, then it evaluates to `length` number of arguments to the script starting from the `offset` position.
${!prefix*} ${!prefix@}	All variables names beginning with `prefix`
${!var[@]} ${!var[*]}	All indexes of array variable `var`
${#var}	Length of value of `var`
${var#drop}	Value of `var` after removing minimum prefix matches of the pattern [14] `drop`
${var##drop}	Value of `var` after removing maximum prefix matches of the pattern `drop`

```bash
st="hello 123"


# Echoes hello 123 (minimal match)
echo ${st#*([a-z])}
```

```
# Echoes ello 123
echo ${st#+([a-z])}

# Echoes 123 (maximum match)
echo ${st##*([a-z])}
```

${var%drop}	Value of `var` after removing minimum suffix matches of the pattern drop
${var%%drop}	Value of `var` after removing maximum suffix matches of the pattern drop
${var^letter}	Changes first letter of `var` to uppercase if it matches `letter` (any alphabet, * or ?)
	If `letter` is not specified, all first letter(s) of `var` will be changed to uppercase
${var^^letter}	Changes any letter of `var` to uppercase if it matches `letter` (any alphabet, * or ?)
	If `letter` is not specified, all letter(s) of `var` will be changed to uppercase
${var,letter}	Changes first letter of `var` to lowercase if it matches `letter` (any alphabet, * or ?)
	If `letter` is not specified, all first letter(s) of `var` will be changed to lowercase
${var,,letter}	Changes any letter of `var` to lowercase if it matches `letter` or * or ?
	If `letter` is not specified, all letter(s) of `var` will be changed to lowercase
${var/find/replace}	Replaces first instance of pattern `find` in `var` with `replace`. If `find` begins with '#', then a match is made at the beginning. A '%' makes it match at the end.
${var//find/replace}	Same as above except that ALL instances of `find` are replaced with `replace`.

- **Arithmetic operations:** Because we need to be very confused.

```
# Outputs 2
echo $(( 1+1 ))

# Sets to 1
a=1

# Increments to 2
let a=a+1
```

```
# Outputs 2
echo $a
```

☞ Beware of the `let` command's return status. It returns 1 if the last argument evaluates to zero and 0 if it does not. If you are assigning the value 0 to a variable, it will not create an error condition. However, the `let` command's exit code will look like there was an error.

Suppose that you are checking if a variable has been assigned a valid number.

```
let a=abc
# Exit code is 1 because abc does not evaluate as a valid
# arithmetic expression and a is assigned 0.


let a=12
# Exit code is 0 because 12 is valid and a is assigned 12.


let a=0
# Exit code is 1 because 0 evaluates to 0. It seems not to be
# a valid arithmetic expression and a is assigned 0.
```

IMHO, this seems like a bad decision on the part of the `bash` creators. If you know better, please let me know. Another problem with `bash` arithmetic is that it is limited to integers and has no overflow protection. In other words, it cannot do decimals. You have to use the interactive `bc` command with `-l` option. For example, if you try to find the value of PI (φ) up to 4 decimal places:

```
~/Desktop
$ a=22 ; let a=a/7 ; echo $a
3


~/Desktop
$ a=22 ; echo "scale=4 ; print $a / 7" | bc -l
3.1428
```

- **awk:** I use `awk` only to cut values from a column. The syntax is C-like. The rest of its functionality is too much to remember. This is all I need to remember.

  ```
  # Prints filenames ($9) newer than the 20th date ($7)
  ls -l | awk ' $7 > 20 { print $9 }'
  ```

- **cut:** I have been using `awk` like this for a long time until I learned that there is a dedicated command to cut columns of text.

  ```
  # Displays 2022-09-29 09:49:09 IST (UTC+0530)
  date +"%Y-%m-%d %T %Z (UTC%z)"


  # Displays 2022
  date +"%Y-%m-%d %T %Z (UTC%z)" | cut -d "-" -f1
  ```

- **Regular expressions in `sed`:** When I tried to use some of my RegEx staples with `sed`, I ran into errors. Apparently, `sed` supports only a subset of RegEx functions. Check its documentation to avoid otherwise intractable problems.

- **Library of functions or include files:** You can place oft-used shell routines as 'functions' in a separate file. You can 'include' this file in your shell scripts simply by placing its pathname after a dot (.). It executes the include file using the current shell instance.

```
. ~/MyShellScripts/MyShellLibrary.txt
```

Inside this file, your functions can be declared in a barebones fashion. Any values pass to the function will be referred as $1, $2,... Any values that you return... No, you cannot return values. Instead, you set a variable and 'export' it. For this reason, it is important to extensively document your include file.

For example, my library file **lib.txt** contains:

```
####################
## Adds two numbers and sets the total to
## variable iADDFN
####################
Add() {
  # Perform the addition and set a variable
  let iADDFN=$1+$2

  # Export the variable
  export iADDFN
}
```

In my other scripts, I include the library of functions file like this:

```
# Include the library file
. lib.txt

# Execute a function from the library file
Add 1 1

# Display the variable exported by the variable
echo $iADDFN
```

When you call a function or a script, `bash` will expand words in the arguments into separate arguments. You will need to escape them or quote them to preserve strings. For example, consider this script (t.txt):

```
echo "Command-line first argument: $1"

my_func() {
  echo "Function first argument: $1"
}
```

```
my_func $*
```

It breaks up the command-line arguments when the function is called.

```
$ bash t.txt Hello,\ World!
Command-line first argument: Hello, World!
Function first argument: Hello,
```

When you double-quote the arguments (`my_func "$*"`), the strings will not be broken up by the function, that is, no word expansion.

- **Protect your scripts:** Shell scripts are usually given the extension `'.sh'`. This makes them easy targets for malware. Though Linux operating system is not usually targeted by malware writers, do not take the risk. Give the extension `'.txt'` for all your shell scripts and do not set their execution bit (+x). When you want to execute them, run them as a parameter to `bash`. Until when malware writers take the trouble of parsing '.txt' file, your shell scripts will be safe.

- **Where art thou `/dev/null`?:** When you do not want to see the output of a command, you can redirect its *standard output* to `/dev/null`.

```
lecommand > /dev/null
```

If that does not silence the command, then maybe it is outputting to *standard error*, instead of *standard output*. That also can be silenced.

```
lecommand > /dev/null 2> /dev/null
```

There is another way of doing the same. It redirects both standard output and standard error to `/dev/null`.

```
lecommand &> /dev/null
```

Similarly, you can log all output to a file.

```
lecommand &> all-out.txt
```

- **Use `printf` instead of `echo`:** Although the `echo` command can be made to accept special characters, a simpler alternative is `printf`.

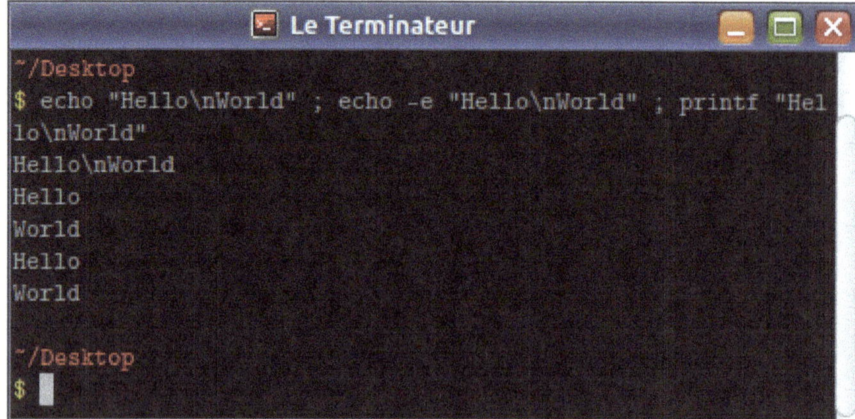

- **Display notifications:** echo need not be the only way to output information. You can also use `notify-send`. It requires two parameters - a title and the message.

```
notify-send "Le Message" "Hello, World!"
```

- **Delay a task:** You can delay the execution of a line in your script using the `sleep` command.

```
sleep 10
read -p "Press Enter to quit" oNothing
```

A better way to do repeated tasks is to schedule them with the `at` command.

- **Here document:** This a temporary text file that you can create and also type out its lines as content, all within a command. It is usually redirected as input for the command. Its format is:

```
some_command <<[-] delimiter
line content
line content
...
line content
delimiter
```

The *Here document* is used with `some_command` that is expecting text content from its standard input. The `delimiter` marks the beginning of the lines of the Here document. The second `delimiter` marks the end of the here doc. It should be on an independent line and with no other content before or after it on the line. The hyphen (`-`) after the redirection operator `<<` is optional. It can be used to make `bash` remove tabs (shown in the next code snippet as →) in the beginning of the lines containing Here document before redirecting it as input to `some_command`.

```
if true; then
→espeak <<- EOF
→Hello World
→EOF
fi
```

- **Use a GUI widget for elevated privileges:** If you run a shell script that uses a `sudo` command (for elevated privileges) and are simultaneously working in another workspace, then the script might just wait forever for you to enter the password. In older versions of Ubuntu, you could use `gksudo` in place of sudo so that you could be prompted for the `sudo` password using a GUI dialog box even if you are in a different workspace.

```
gksudo whatever-command-you-want-to-run-with-its-arguments
```

In newer versions of Ubuntu, gksu and gksudo have been dropped. The alternative now is pkexec command.

```
pkexec env DISPLAY=$DISPLAY XAUTHORITY=$XAUTHORITY
whatever-command-you-want-to-run-with-its-arguments
```

I have this .bashrc alias...

```
alias ssu='pkexec env DISPLAY=$DISPLAY XAUTHORITY=$XAUTHORITY'
```

... so that I can do the same as above but with less typing.

```
ssu whatever-command-you-want-to-run-with-its-arguments
```

If you are typing the command for an application launcher, then just pkexec can be used as a drop-in replacement for gksudo, that is, without all the display and xauthority thingamajigs.

- **Use GUI widgets for prompts:** I do not just write, illustrate and design my books; I also build them as ebooks and PDFs using scripts. The zenity command can be used to display several kinds of GUI dialogs from shell scripts. To build this book, I use this command in my 'book-building script'.

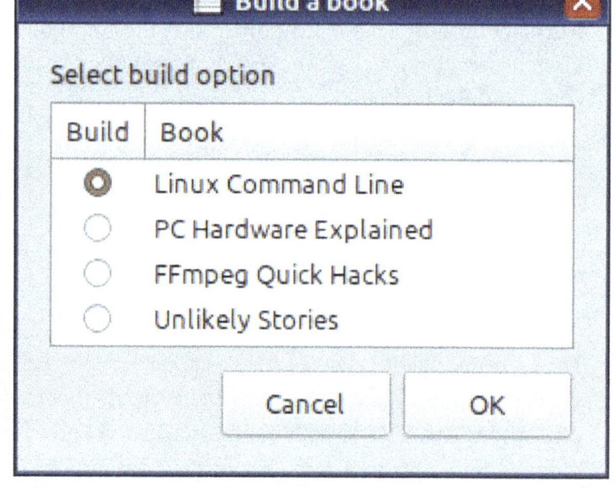


```
sBook=$(zenity -
-title "Build a
book" --text "Select
build option" --list
--radiolist --column
"Build" --column
"Book" True 'Linux
Command Line' FALSE 'PC Hardware Explained')
```

- **Cut from the middle:** You can use head to take the top off a text file and tail to take the bottom. How to take the middle?

```
# Print one line next to and in addition to line 6
sed -n '6+1p' list.txt


# Deletes lines from 6 to 8 and save changes to the file
sed -i "6,8d" list.txt
```

- **Beware of undefined variables:** What happens when the variable $some_dir has not yet been defined and you try sudo rm -rf $some_dir/? NO, DO NOT TRY IT! It will try to delete your entire file system. bash will replace the non-existent $some_dir variable with an empty string and consider your command as sudo rm -rf /. Is that what you want? Thankfully, you can protect your scripts by beginning them like this:

```bash
#!/bin/bash
set -u

# your script code
```

- **Handle errors or stop execution**: If your shell scripts do not have any parsing errors, then `bash` will execute the statements from start to finish, one after the other, without any interruption. If any command encounters any error, `bash` will display its error and proceed to the next statement. It is entirely your responsibility to handle all errors. You can use `if [ $? -eq 0 ]; then` to check if the previous command has executed successfully and then proceed with other statements. You can also daisy-chained commands [15] using the && (AND logical operator) to ensure that commands are executed only if previous commands are successful. What if you do not want to nest all your commands in multiple `if` statements or stringify them with the &&? Well, you can use the `set -e` option to make the shell stop the execution of the script when a command exits with an non-zero error code. To combine with the previous set command, you can begin your shell scripts like this:

```bash
#!/bin/bash
set -eu

# your script code
```

How do you handle error conditions after the `set -e` option? Use the || logical operator between the required command to be tested and the error handler command. If the command on the left of the || operator succeeds without an error, then the error handler command will not be executed. You can wrap multi-line commands inside brackets.

```bash
# Outputs This echo will never fail
echo "This echo will never fail." || echo "The echo failed."

# Outputs Hello and World
(echo Hello &&
 echo World ) || echo "The echoes failed"

# Outputs include Some command failed
(echo Hello &&
 rm NoSuchDir &&
 echo World ) || echo "Some command failed"
```

- **Escaping**: You can escape
  - special characters using the backslash (\ ). To escape the backslash character, use double backslashes (\\ ).
  - literal text strings by wrapping them in single quotation marks (' '). Bash will not perform any expansions or substitutions. The single-quoted string should not have any more single-quotation marks. Bash will not perform any backslash-escaping either.

- literal text strings by wrapping them in double-quotation marks (" ") but allowing for
    - $-prefixed variables, expansions and substitutions
    - backslash-escaped characters
    - backquoted (` `) command strings
    - history-expansion character

```
# Displays Hello World
a=World; echo "Hello $a"

# Displays Hello $a
a=World; echo 'Hello $a'

# Displays Hello 'World'
a=World; echo "Hello '$a'"
```

- **Printer's error**: The *Bash Reference Manual* and many printed documentation use wrong characters for the quotation marks. The *apostrophe* or u+0027 used in single-quoted strings may be replaced with the *right single quotation mark* or u+2019. The grave accent or u+0060 used in backquoted strings may be replaced with *left single quotation mark* or u+2018. The *quotation mark* or u+0022 used in double-quoted strings may also be replaced with left and right double quotation marks. They look similar but will result in an error if used in a shell script or in the command-line. I write my books in CommonMark (MarkDown) and directly output them as ePUB ebook and printable PDF documents. They will not have such errors. (There may be other errors.) When someone edits a document (before it goes to print) in a rich-text editor such as LibreOffice or Microsoft Office, the editor's autocorrect feature may change ordinary quotation marks and backquotes with inverted quotation marks. Just be aware that this can happen. Just type the commands. Do not copy-paste.

- **Your own secret scripting mimetype**: I do not use the `.sh` extension for my shell scripts. Neither do I give the `+x` (execute) permission for them. Even though Linux systems are not plagued by viruses, you can never be too careful. For several years, my scripts remained anonymous with a `.txt`. Eventually, I got tired and created a special file type with a new extension of my choice `.sh.txt`. For this, I created a mimetype definition file (special-bash-script-text-mime.xml).

```xml
<?xml version="1.0"?>
<mime-info xmlns="http://www.freedesktop.org/standards/shared-mime-info">
  <mime-type type="text/bash-script-text">
   <comment>Special bash script text document</comment>
   <glob pattern="*.sh.txt"/>
  </mime-type>
</mime-info>
```

The new mimetype `text/bash-script-text` was from my imagination and I installed it with the command:

```
xdg-mime install special-bash-script-text-mime.xml
```

Then, I created a Caja Actions Configuration [32] with the criteria filter for the new mimetype. Now, if I click on a `.sh.txt` file, it open in a text editor like any other text file. When required, I can run/launch the script with `/usr/bin/bash` by using a context menu (right-click menu) option inside the Caja file manager or on the Mate desktop.

Caja Actions Configuration

In Gnome 2, the file manager Nautilus could be optimized by adding your own scripts to its context menus. In Gnome 3, the entire desktop down was dumbed down to make it more likeable for ~~herd followers~~ Mac converts. Imitating the Apple philosophy, Gnome 3 designers do not want their users modifying their precious ~~good-for-nothing~~ desktop. Unlike the ~~sheep~~ fanboys who obsequiously accepted Gnome 3, many other users like me switched to the Mate desktop, which follows the Gnome 2 philosophy of freedom and respect for users.

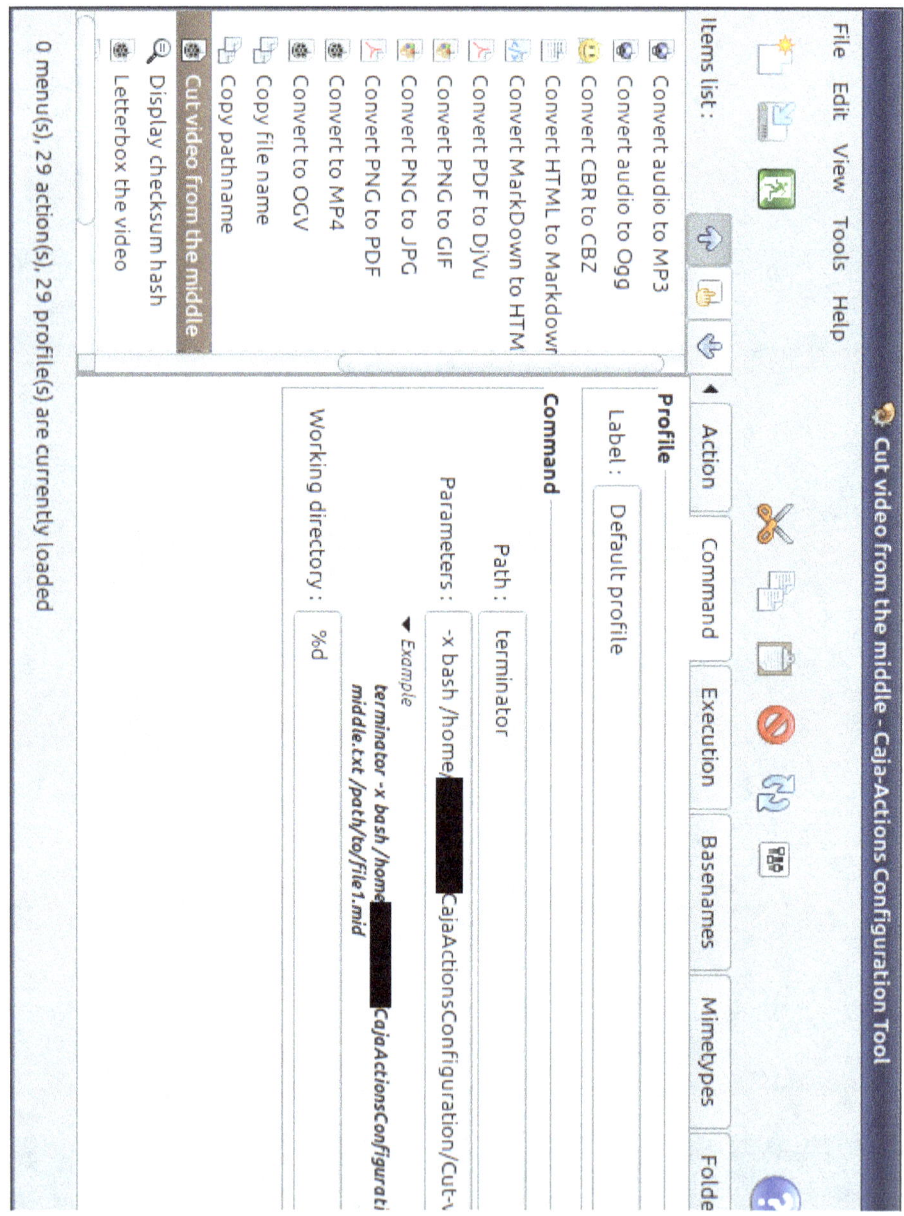

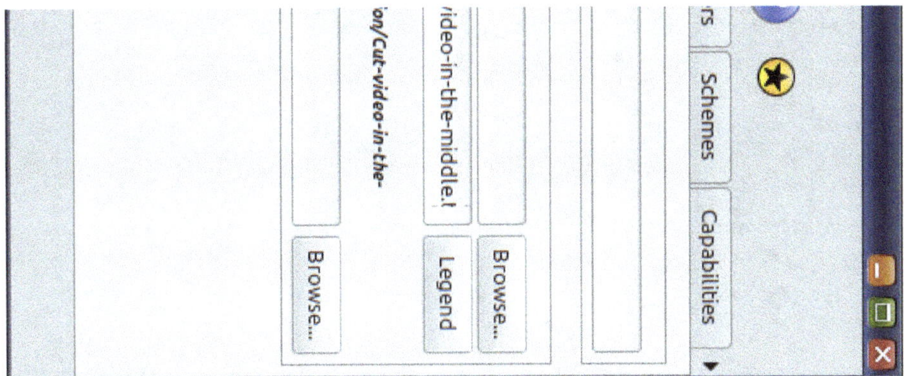

Here are some context menus that you can use.

- **Copy filename:**

```
# Name:           Copy filename
# Description:    Copy the file name to clipboard
# Command:        bash
# Arguments:      Copy-Filename.txt %b


xsel --clear
echo -e "$1\c" | xclip -selection clipboard
if [ $? -eq 0 ]; then
  notify-send "Copied" "$1"
else
  notify-send "Copy Failed" "$?"
fi
```

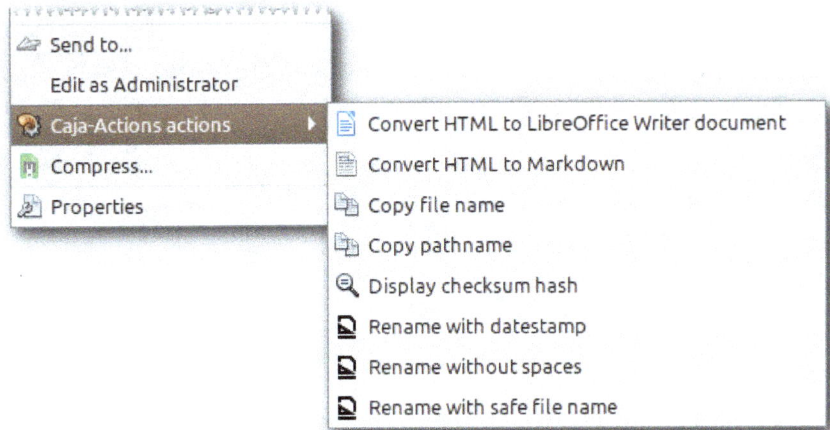

- **Copy pathname:**

```
# Name:           Copy pathname
# Description:    Copy the path of this file to clipboard
```

```
# Command:          bash
# Arguments:        Copy-Pathname.txt %f

xsel --clear
echo -e "$1\c" | xclip -selection clipboard
if [ $? -eq 0 ]; then
  notify-send "Copied" "$1"
else
  notify-send "Copy Failed" "$?"
fi
```

On my website, I have made available a copy path/name utility for Windows. It is very old but it should work on all versions of Windows. Complete source code is also available on the site.

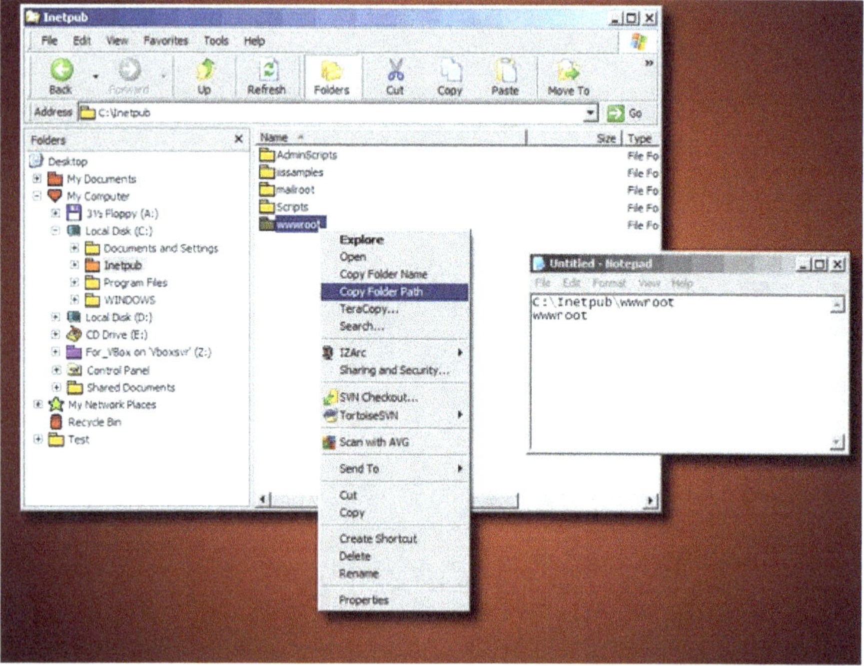

- **Rename a file with the datestamp:** If you need to store invoices and other historical documents, retrieving them by date is easier with timestamps in the names.

```
# Name:             Rename with datestamp
# Description:      Suffixes datestamp to the name of this file
# Command:          terminator
# Arguments:        -x bash Rename-with-datestamp.txt %f
# Conditions:       Basename matching *.?* AND
#                   Mimetype matching * AND
#                           NOT matching inode/directory
# Environment:      Count = 1
```

```bash
sFile="$*"

if [ -d "$sFile" ]; then
  echo "Skipped: Directory - $sFile"
else
  sDirectory=$(dirname "$sFile")
  sFilename=$(basename "$sFile")
  sFilename="${sFilename%.*}"
  sFileExtension="${sFile##*.}"

  sDateStamp=$(ls -l --time-style=full-iso "$sFile" | \
              awk -F [.\ :] '{print $6"_"$7$8"-"$9}' )


sOutputFile="${sDirectory}/${sFilename}_${sDateStamp}.${sFileExten
sion}"

  mv "$sFile" "$sOutputFile"
  if [ $? -eq 0 ]; then
    notify-send "SUCCESS: Renaming" "$sOutputFile"
    echo "SUCCESS: Renaming to $sOutputFile"
  else
    notify-send "FAILURE: Renaming" "$sFile"
    echo "FAILURE: Renaming $sFile"
    read -p "Press Enter to quit" oNothing
  fi
fi
```

- **Silence a video:** A lot of online videos have very annoying music. I prefer to watch
  them in silence. Control-freak much?

```bash
# Name:        Silence the video
# Description: Remove sound stream from the video file
# Command:     terminator
# Arguments:   -x bash Silence-the-video.txt %f
# Mimetype:    video/*

sFile="$*"
sOutputFile="${sFile%.*}-SILENT.mp4"


ffmpeg -y -i "$sFile" -codec copy -an "$sOutputFile"


if [ $? -eq 0 ]; then
  notify-send "Audio removal complete" "$sOutputFile"
else
  notify-send "Audio removal failed" "$sFile"
```

```
    read -p "Press Enter to quit" oNothing
fi
```

- **Encrypt a PDF with a password:** When you send important documents to others, it is better to encrypt it with a password.

```
# Name:           Set PDF password
# Description:    Encrypts a PDF with given password
# Command:        terminator
# Arguments:      -x bash Set-PDF-password.txt %f
# Mimetype:       application/pdf
# Environment:    Count = 1


sFile="$*"
sFileName=$(basename "$sFile")


sOutputFileName="${sFile%.*}-ENCRYPTED.pdf"


sPassword=$(zenity --password --title "Encrypt PDF" \
                --text "Type the password")


if [ -z $sPassword ]; then
  notify-send "ABANDONED: Password encryption" "$sFileName"
  echo "ABANDONED: Password encryption - $sFileName"
else
  # sOsWsNhEhRiPtAsSsSeWcOrReDt is the owner password.
  # Change it and make it a secret.
  # Reveal only the typed-in passwords to recipients.
  qpdf --encrypt "$sPassword" "sOsWsNhEhRiPtAsSsSeWcOrReDt" \
      256 --print=none -- "$sFile" "$sOutputFileName"
  if [ $? -eq 0 ]; then
    notify-send "SUCCESS: Password encryption" "$sOutputFileName"
    echo "SUCCESS: Password encryption - $sOutputFileName"
  else
    notify-send "FAILURE: Password encryption" "$sFileName"
    echo "FAILURE: Password encryption - $sFileName"
  fi
fi


read -p "Press Enter to quit" oNothing
```

To decrypt a password-protected PDF, I use a similar script, as listed in a later chapter. [75]

System Administration

- **List only directories**: In Microsoft DOS, you can list directories in the current path with the command `dir /ad`. In `bash`, the `ls` command does not have an equivalent option. You can use `ls -d */` but it will append a forward slash (/) to the name of each directory. Strangely, the `find` command rather than the `ls` command is able to do the needful.

```
find * -maxdepth 0 -type d
```

- **Schedule tasks:** You can schedule tasks for later using the `at` command. (Some genius has removed it from Ubuntu. You can install it back with `sudo apt-get install at`.)

```
at -f ~/reminders.txt 5:55
```

The `at` command runs the script file using the old Bourne shell (`sh`) so use the hashbang comment (`#!/bin/bash`) at the top of the script.

- **Run tasks after a delay:**

```
sleep 120 && notify-send "Hello" "Take a break" &
```

- **Move files to the Trash:** Unlike the desktop trash command, the console `rm` command permanently deletes a file. How do you programmatically move files to the trash?

```
if [ $# -gt 0 ]; then
  for sFile in "$@"
  do
    if [ -f "$sFile" ];then
      sFilename=$(basename "$sFile")
      sDirname=$(dirname "$sFile")
      if [[ $sDirname = "." ]]; then
        sDirname=$(pwd)
      fi
      sPathname="${sDirname}/${sFilename}"

      sTempFileInfo="/tmp/${sFilename}.trashinfo"
      echo "[Trash Info]" > "$sTempFileInfo"
      echo "Path=${sPathname}" >> "$sTempFileInfo"
      echo "DeletionDate=$(date +"%Y-%m-%dT%T")" \
          >> "$sTempFileInfo"
      mv "$sTempFileInfo" "${HOME}/.local/share/Trash/info"

      mv -f "$sFile" ${HOME}/.local/share/Trash/files

      if [ $? -eq 0 ]; then
        echo "SUCCESS: Deleting $sFile"
      else
```

```
        echo "FAILURE: Deleting $sFile"
      fi
    else
      echo "ABANDONED: $sFile not found"
    fi
  done
else
  echo "ABANDONED: No files specified"
fi
```

☞ In some distros, `$USER` may be available as `$USERNAME`. If all that you want to do is access the 'home' directory of the current user, then just use `$HOME`.

- **Delete files forever**: When you delete files, the file name may be removed from the list of contents in the directory but the file contents may remain on the disc. Use the command `shred` to scramble the contents (fill the file with random junk data) and then manually delete the file. If someone uses data recovery programs to retrieve such files, they will not find the original data. This program is great for FAT-formatted portable disk drives but may not be useful on file systems that have mirroring or other redundancy features. This includes ext3 and ext4 drives that are typically used in Linux.

  By default, `shred` will overwrite file contents with random data three times. With the `-zero` option, `shred` will overwrite the file with zero values, after the overwrites with random values. If you want to quickly zero the data, use `-zero` option but set the `--iterations` option to zero.

  ```
  cd /media/ya-username/USB1/TopSecretData
  find * -type f -exec shred --zero --iterations 0 -v '{}' \;
  rm -rf *
  ```

- **Find the full path of a file**: Sometimes, your scripts will have to process relative pathnames. How do you find their absolute file names?

  ```
  # Outputs /home/me/Desktop/somefile.txt for me
  readlink -f ./somefile.txt
  ```

- **Hard vs. soft links**: When you create a soft link (`ln -s target linkname`), you are create a proxy for a file. If the original file gets delete, the link becomes broken. When you create a hard link (ln target linkname), the underlying data remains the same for both. Even if the target gets deleted, the new link survives.

- **Recursively delete files or directories**: You can use the `-delete` option of the `find` command to recursively wade through a directory and delete matching files.

  ```
  # Deletes hidden files '.uuid'
  find some-font-dir -type f -name '.uid' -delete
  ```

  To delete directories, they need to be empty. An alternative is to use its `-exec` option to launch the `rm` command on the found directories.

  ```
  find ./Android/SubhashBrowser \
      -type d -name '.svn' \
      -exec rm -rf '{}' \;
  ```

The -exec option accepts any command. It will replace {} with the name of the found file or directory. To prevent it from being interpreted by shell as a brace expansion, it is quoted as '{}'. The command passed to the -exec option must be terminated with a semi-colon. To prevent the semicolon from being interpreted as a command separator, it is escaped as \;.

- **System Cleanup:** I have a script in which I have a list of directories that need to be regularly cleaned up. Browsers hide a ton of files. Deleting them frees a lot of space.

```
echo "Emptying desktop trash"
rm -rf $HOME/.local/share/Trash/*
rm -rf $HOME/.local/share/tracker/*

echo "Emptying other trash directories"
arFolders=('/home/user/.mozilla/firefox/profile-dir/crashes' \
    '/home/user/.mozilla/firefox/profile-dir/datareporting' \
    '/home/user/.mozilla/firefox/profile-dir/minidumps' \
    '/home/user/.mozilla/firefox/profile-dir/sessionstore-backups' \
    '/home/user/.mozilla/firefox/profile-dir/weave' \
    '/home/user/.cache' '/home/user/.thumbnails')

for sFolder in "${arFolders[@]}"
do
  echo "Deleting ${sFolder}/*.*"
  rm -rf "${sFolder}/*"
done
```

To clear temporary files created by system process, you need to run this script with root privileges.

```
# Delete temporary files older than a day
find /var/backups/* -atime +1 -type f -delete
find /var/tmp/* -atime +1 -type f -delete
find /tmp/* -atime +1 -type f -delete

echo "Reducing journal logs"
journalctl --vacuum-size=50M
```

☞ I have used /var/backups only as an example. On my computer, this directory can be safely deleted. On an another computer, it may not be so. Deleting directories with root privileges requires proper care and judgement. This is the reason I do not provide these commands in a text file. I want you understand the ideas, not copy-paste commands blindly.

☞ I do not understand why people do not realize what a crappy spyware browser Google Chrome is. Uninstall it. It will save you a lot of space. Your computer will run faster as the browser is a bandwidth and CPU hog.

- **Run as root:** Root is like the *Administrator* account in Microsoft Windows. Because the root has full permissions on the system, mistakes can be very destructive. For this reason, the root account is not available for ordinary users. Instead, ordinary users can temporarily acquire root privileges by providing the username and password of an account that has root privileges.

In most Linux distributions, the first user account that you create during installation is given root privileges by default. For safety reasons, this account ordinarily runs with limited privileges or permissions. When root privileges are required, such as when installing applications or partitioning the hard disk, this user will be prompted to provide the password. In Ubuntu and other distributions, sudo is the means with which the default user accounts temporarily runs commands with root privileges. For example:

```
sudo fdisk -l
```

If the default user types just `fdisk -l`, then the command runs with limited privileges and will not be able to detect all partitions.

The sudo word refers to the su command, which was traditionally used to access the root account. If you typed `'sudo sh'`, you will be able to access the root shell. The prompt will turn to # indicating that you are now running the shell as root.

- **Startup programs:** The Mate desktop provides an app under the menu *System » Preferences » Personal » Startup Applications* to let you add applications to the startup. While you could create symbolic links (`ln -s`) for your startup programs in the folder `~/.config/autostart`, the app seems to provide more control. You can specify extra settings such as delay.

- **Run in the background:** You can run a command in the background by ending the command with a space and an ampersand.

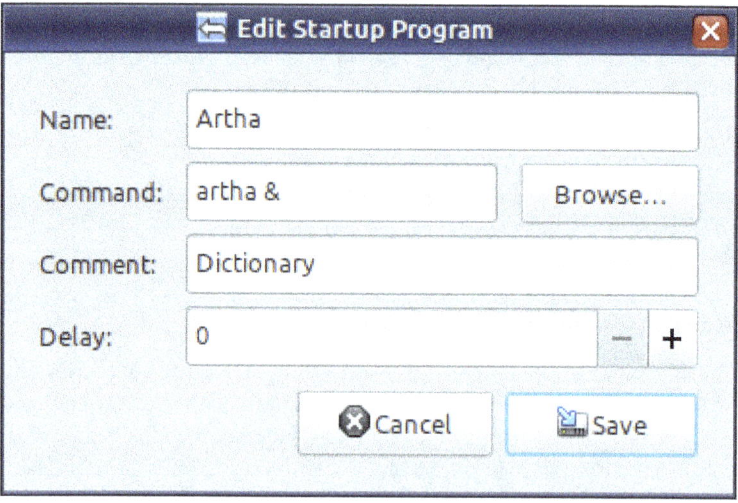

The Artha dictionary application moves to the system tray instead of displaying its window if you start it in the background.

- **Run in the background without getting killed:** Sometimes programs added to startup get killed prematurely. Start them with the *no hangup* command.

```
nohup bash start-netcheck.txt > /tmp/netcheck_nohup_out.log 2> /tmp/netcheck_nohup_err.log &
```

Even this does not save my Java app. The JVM takes quite some time to load. I add a `sleep 6` after the above command so that the JVM loads all right. Here is an old knock-knock joke about Java.

> Knock! Knock!
>
> Who is there?
>
> *(after a delay)* Java.

Although this joke is not in my jokebook, I have written two whole chapters of tech jokes - *Computer Jokes* and *Computer Programming Jokes*.

Check the `--help` or `--help-all` output to list all parameters of an application. There *may* be a built-in option for running the application as a dæmon (background process) natively.

```
/usr/sbin/firestarter --start-hidden
```

- **Run as another user:** While being logged in as one user and needing to run as another user, use the `su` command.

  ```
  su user2
  ```

- **Force update with Internet time servers:** Usually, the NTP dæmon ensures that your computer's time is synchronised with Internet timeservers. This need not happen every time you start your computer. Once synchronised the time is stored in the RTC clock of the BIOS and preserved by the BIOS battery on the motherboard. So, I change the setting to *manual* after synchronization. When the battery becomes old or if you misconfigured something, then you may need to synchronise with the timeservers again. This can take its own sweet time. However, you can force it to get on time.

  ```
  sudo ntpdate -b swisstime.ethz.ch
  ```

- **Change GRUB2 wallpaper:** The GRUB2 boot menu is created from a shell script masquerading as a configuration file /boot/grub/grub.cfg. It is created by some other scripts in the /etc/grubd directory. Linux distributions have been changing the scripts so often that any trick to customize the wallpaper will become obsolete quickly. The surefire solution is to modify the grub.cfg file directly after it has been updated by sudo update-grub. You have to directly rely on Grub commands and environment variables. In the section where the grub theme details are specified, I add this content:

```
...

# Colour variables are set as foreground/background.
# Background set to black means transparent.
# Foreground set to black means black.
# Colour options are black, blue, brown, cyan,
# dark-gray, green, light-cyan, light-blue,
# light-green, light-gray, light-magenta, light-red,
# magenta, red, white, yellow

set menu_colour_normal=light-red/black
set menu_colour_highlight=white/black

background_image "/opt/Wallpapers/BG_Sabayon.jpg"
### END /etc/grub.d/05_debian_theme ###
```

The *grub.cfg* file is not meant to be edited by the end-user. So, anytime you update grub (such as when a new kernel is installed), your grub.cfg modifications will be lost. You will have to redo them again.

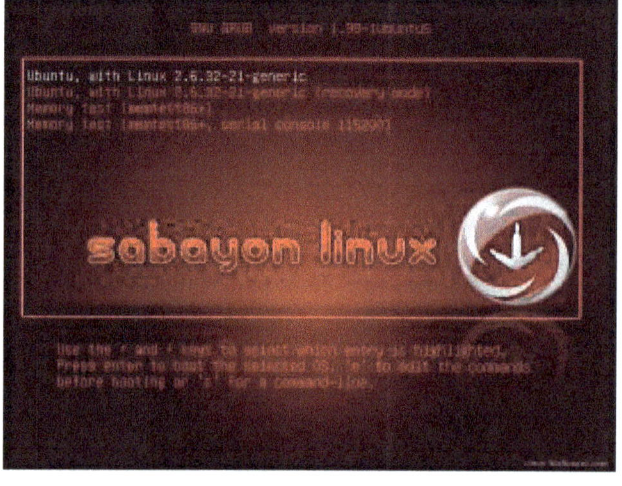

- **Restore GRUB using chroot jail:** After over a decade with an old Ubuntu OS, I installed Mint 20 to a new partition. Although, it added the old Grub menu in a submenu, it froze when I chose the old OS. I had to follow these steps to restore the old Grub to MBR.

  ○ Opened Terminal and listed the numbers of my hard disk partitions.

    ```
    sudo fdisk -l
    ```

  ○ Noted the partition number where I installed Linux. If you have installed the

/boot in another partition, note its number too.

- o Created a directory where I could mount my old file system.

  ```
  sudo mkdir /mnt/test
  ```

- o Mounted the old file system.

  ```
  sudo mount --bind /dev /mnt/test/dev
  sudo mount --bind /proc /mnt/test/proc
  sudo mount --bind /sys /mnt/test/sys
  ```

- o If you have installed /boot to another partition, mount that partition.

  ```
  sudo mount /dev/sdxy /mnt/test/boot
  ```

  Replace y in sdxy with the number of your boot partition. Also replace x with the alphabetical order of the hard disk. This step is not necessary if you do not have a separate boot partition.

- o Logged in to my linux installation as root.

  ```
  sudo chroot /mnt/test
  ```

- o Updated Grub 2 boot menu. There was no need to use sudo as I was logged in as root.

  ```
  update-grub
  ```

- o Restored Grub 2 on the master boot record (MBR).

  ```
  grub-install /dev/sdx
  ```

  I replace x in sdx with the alphabetical order of my hard disk. If you have only one hard disk, then it must be sda.

- o Logged out of my installation by pressing Ctrl+D.
- o Unmounted my file system in the reverse order.

  ```
  sudo umount /mnt/test/sys
  sudo umount /mnt/test/proc
  sudo umount /mnt/test/dev
  sudo umount /mnt/test
  ```

  You need to type sudo umount /boot before unmounting /mnt/test only if you have a separate boot partition.

- o Typed sudo reboot to restart the machine.
- o Removed the Live CD or USB, and was greeted by the old Grub 2 menu.

- **Adjust screen brightness:** The screen on my laptop was replaced after the original stopped working. The computer repair shop did not install the new screen properly and the brightness adjustment applet setting has the exact opposite effect - full brightness makes it dim and dim makes it full brightness. I have to manually set the brightness level every time I login to the computer. I now have command-line alternative.

  ```
  # Lists names of screens and key lock LEDs
  brightnessctl --list
  ```

```
# List information on specified screen
brightnessctl info --device='whatever-screen-name'
```

```
# Set brightness for the screen
brightnessctl set 33% --device='whatever-screen-name'
```

The `brightnessctl` seems to have no effect in new Ubuntu installation. I have to use the `xrandr` command instead.

```
xrandr --output LVDS --brightness 0.6
```

You can type `xrandr -q` to obtain the name of your screen device that you need to use after the `--output` switch. This command replaces the obsolete `xgamma` command as it has a `--gamma` switch.

```
xrandr --output eDP --brightness 0.6 --gamma 1:1:1
```

There are also other commands such as `light` and `xbacklight` that you can try.

- **Reassign mouse button functions:** Sometimes, one of the buttons in a mouse stops working. If it is the right-click button, I would swap its function through software.

  ```
  # Change button map of device #12
  xinput set-button-map 12 1 3 2 4 5 6 7
  ```

Usually, the buttons are mapped like this: Left (1), Scroll (2), Right (3), Scroll Up (4), Scroll Down (5)... To be sure, however, you can study the output generated by the command `xev` in response to your mouse button clicks. If it is the left-click button, I would rather desolder its push button and swap it with that of the right-click button. If you can desolder stuff, then perhaps you might be interested in my book *Cool Electronic Projects.* [98]

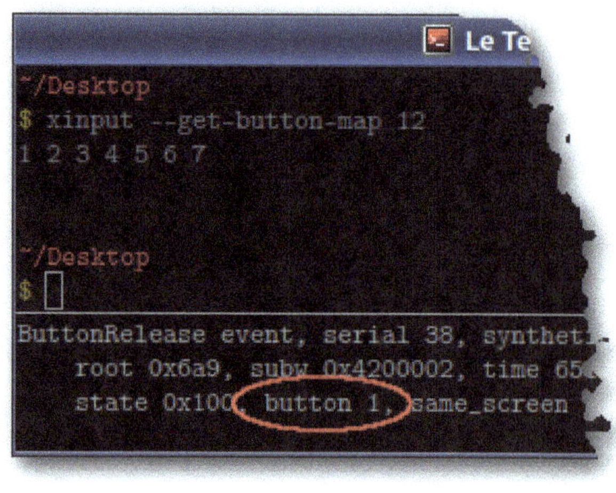

- **Disable touchpad:** If you are a touch-typist, then the touchpad will annoy you. You are better off with an external mouse. You can use the `xinput` command to configure your mouse devices.

  ```
  # List input devices and their numbers
  xinput --list    # lists the mouse as device #12
  ```

  ```
  # List properties of device #12
  xinput --list-props 12
  ```

```
# List button map of device #12
xinput --get-button-map 12


# Disables device #12
xinput --set-prop 12 "Device enabled" 0
```

- **Disable radio devices:** After I get a new laptop, I remove the wireless chip from a bottom panel. (I use wired LAN and I do not trust wireless networks.) I assume this also removes the bluetooth radio. While Linux does not detect these devices any more, their LEDs continue to light up. To ensure that these devices are really off, I installed **tlp**. In the `/etc/tlp.conf` file, I disabled all radio devices.

```
DEVICES_TO_DISABLE_ON_STARTUP="bluetooth wifi wwan"
```

- **Disable webcam:** The webcam and microphone on a laptop can be hacked through the Internet and switched on without the indicator light coming on. For this reason, I put black tape over the webcam and microphone outlets on the screen bezel. Additionally, I have blacklisted the webcam driver by including it in the `/etc/modprobe.d/blacklist.conf` file. If the `uvcvideo` driver is not listed for this command, then the driver has been successfully blacklisted.

```
sudo lsmod | grep uvcvideo
```

To disable the microphone, I do select only an 'output' sound hardware configuration profiles in *Sound Preferences*, never 'input' and 'duplex' ones.

- **Detect device IP in LAN:** Even though I assign static IP addresses to devices such as routers, game consoles and 'smart' TVs, I forget their numbers. I use this script detect their IP. All of these devices run a web server (on port 80) to provide you with a password-protected configuration page. All you need to do now is to check if a particular IP accepts connections on port 80.

```
let iClient=0


while [ $iClient -lt 255 ]; do
  echo "Testing 192.168.0.$iClient"
  nc -zv 192.168.0.$iClient 80
  if [ $? -eq 0 ]; then
    notify-send "LAN IP" "192.168.0.$iClient"
  fi
  let ++iClient;
done
```

- **Use a RAM drive:** In the MS-DOS world, a *RAM drive* is a temporary disk partition created out of the free space in the system RAM (memory). The contents of this space gets lost when the system is shut down. But, when the system is on, the RAM drive provides some fast extra storage space. On my laptop, the memory consumption is just over 600 MB. Much of the 6 GB system RAM that I have is never used. However, I frequently run out of disk space when working with multimedia files. I have added this line in my `/etc/fstab` file to create a 2-GB RAM drive. It is faster than my SSD hard disk.

```
RAMdrive /media/RamDrive tmpfs defaults,size=2G,x-gvfs-show 0 0
```

If I wanted to create a RAM drive without modifying the /etc/fstab file, I would have to first create a directory /media/ma-username/RamDrive and then mount the RAM drive on it:

```
sudo mkdir /media/ma-username/RamDrive
sudo mount -t tmpfs \
           -o size=2048m RAMdrive \
           /media/ma-username/RamDrive
```

To discard the drive, I could simply issue the command sudo umount RAMdrive.

- **Manage tar and gz files:** Tar and gz are archive formats. The gzip command compresses individual files. The files get deleted and are replaced by their complement of .gz files. You can run the gunzip command to restore the files.

```
~/Desktop/FasDrive
$ ls
cover-lcltt-3d.png  cover-lcltt-back.png  cover-lcltt-front.png
term.png


~/Desktop/FasDrive
$ gzip *


~/Desktop/FasDrive
$ ls
cover-lcltt-3d.png.gz    cover-lcltt-front.png.gz
cover-lcltt-back.png.gz  term.png.gz


~/Desktop/FasDrive
$ gunzip *


~/Desktop/FasDrive
$ ls
cover-lcltt-3d.png  cover-lcltt-back.png  cover-lcltt-front.png
term.png
```

The tar command behaves like the Windows 'compressed folder' feature. It can work on multiple files and creates one .tar.gz file. It does not delete the original files. The *tar* command can be used to extract the archive as well.

```
~/Desktop/FasDrive
$ ls
cover-lcltt-3d.png  cover-lcltt-back.png  cover-lcltt-front.png
term.png


~/Desktop/FasDrive
```

```
$ tar -czf cover-images.tar.gz *.png


~/Desktop/FasDrive
$ ls
cover-images.tar.gz    cover-lcltt-back.png    term.png
cover-lcltt-3d.png     cover-lcltt-front.png


~/Desktop/FasDrive
$ rm *.png


~/Desktop/FasDrive
$ ls
cover-images.tar.gz


~/Desktop/FasDrive
$ tar -xf cover-images.tar.gz


~/Desktop/FasDrive
$ ls
cover-images.tar.gz    cover-lcltt-back.png    term.png
cover-lcltt-3d.png     cover-lcltt-front.png
```

This is fine if the files you want to archive are in the current directory. When you try
to archive files in another directory, tar annoyingly includes all parent directories
starting from root (/). To create the archive without changing directories, use the -C
option to make tar to internally change to the parent of the target directory.

```
# Compress directory $HOME/Pictures/Wallpapers directory
tar -acf wallpapers.tar.gz -C ~/Pictures Wallpapers
```

When you use the -C option, ensure that the names of input files/directories (the
last set of arguments) is explicitly specified. Wildcards will not work because it is the
shell that expands them, not tar.

```
# Compress all PNG files in the $HOME/Pictures directory
tar -acf pictures.tar.gz -C ~/Pictures \
    $(cd ~/Pictures ; ls *.png)


# This will not work:
# tar -acf pictures.tar.gz -C ~/Pictures *.png
```

Pipe afficianados can instead use the find command if they like to complicate
things. To prevent find from outputting the full path and to delimit each file name
with a new line or the line feed character, its -printf option needs to be used. To
process this formatted output, tar will require the -T option. The final hyphen
option of the tar command draws the names of input files over the pipe from the
find command.

```
find ~/Pictures/*.png -printf '%f\n' | \
   tar -acf img.tar.gz -C ~/Pictures -T -
```

- **apt, aptitude or apt-get:** Do they remind you of *Ed, Edd n Eddy*? My distro of choice is Ubuntu. In Ubuntu, software management operations can be performed using `apt`, `apt-get`, `aptitude` or `dpkg`. `dpkg` seems to be the dumbest of the lot. It does one thing and it does that right. Traditionally, most Ubuntu guides have recommended `apt-get`. Now, they recommend `apt` or `aptitude`. The syntax is similar. `apt` is friendlier than `apt-get` and definitely eliminates a lot of keystrokes. Recently, I could not install a package. The `apt-get` error message implied that I had broken packages. I opened Synaptic Package Manager and found no broken packages. Then, instead of `'sudo apt-get install'`, I tried `'sudo aptitude install'`. The `aptitude` command stated exactly what was wrong, what alternative could be tried and installed the correct package after I followed its recommendation. Obviously, `aptitude` is the better choice. It seems to have the best attitude.

- **Build from source:** What do you do when your distro no longer packages your favourite program? Build from source! Download the source files and follow the instructions in the readme file. The steps are usually like this.

```
cd /directory-of-extracted-source
./configure
sudo make
sudo make install
```

You may run into some errors in `./configure` step. It might complain that some package is missing or too old. Use your software manager app to install/upgrade such packages and try again. Eventually, everything will be installed fine and dandy.

- **Text files off the Internet** : Microsoft Windows is the scumbag among operating systems. (I know you Android haters want to say that Android is worse but I think Microsoft has been in this game much longer. Billie boy stole DOS from CP/M and Windows NT from DEC VMS before Android creators were even born so some respect please. ... Android was stolen from Java? So is C#. *Touché*? Duffy's Tavern?) Well, Windows creates text files with lines ending in CR (carriage return — 0x0D — \r) and LF (line feed — 0x0A — \n) while Unices end lines with just LF. If you know that a text file that was downloaded from the Internet was created in Windows...

```
$ head ~/Downloads/http_proxies.txt | hexdump -C | head -3
00000000  31 31 37 2e 31 36 30 2e  32 35 30 2e 31 33 37 3a  |117.160.250.137:|
00000010  38 30 0d 0a 38 31 2e 36  39 2e 31 37 31 2e 31 35  |80..81.69.171.15|
00000020  39 3a 32 30 38 30 0d 0a  33 31 2e 31 32 38 2e 31  |9:2080..31.128.1|
```

... then, be sure to replace CR-LF line-endings with just LF.

```
sed -i 's/\r$//' http_proxies.txt
```

```
$ head http_proxies.txt | hexdump -C | head -3
00000000  31 31 37 2e 31 36 30 2e  32 35 30 2e 31 33 37 3a  |117.160.250.137:|
00000010  38 30 0a 38 31 2e 36 39  2e 31 37 31 2e 31 35 39  |80.81.69.171.159|
00000020  3a 32 30 38 30 0a 33 31  2e 31 32 38 2e 31 33 30  |:2080.31.128.130|
```

- **Wine Prefixes**: By default, `wine` is configured to run 64-bit Windows applications. If

the Windows software that you want to run are 16-bit or 32-bit programs of yore, you
need to create a Wine prefix for them. This is a special directory for those software.

```
WINEARCH=win32 WINEPREFIX="${HOME}/MyWine32Prefix" winecfg
```

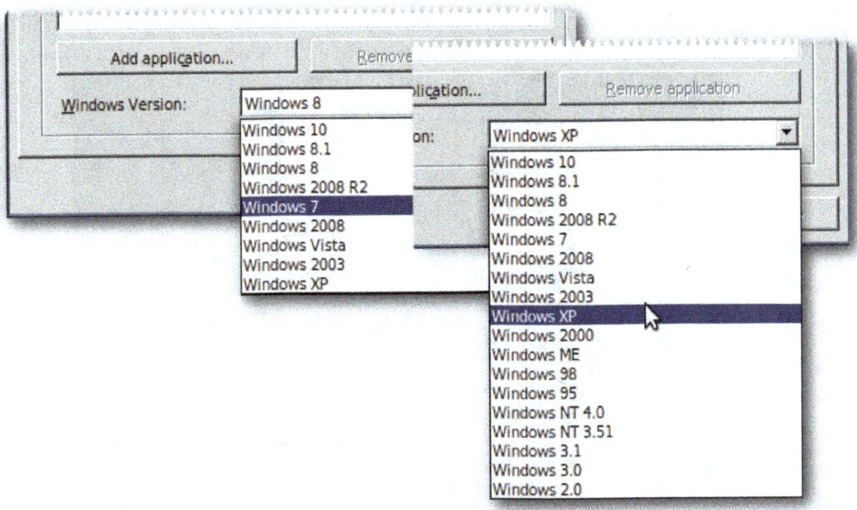

This new directory will prevent Wine from contaminating the 64-bit prefix directory
that it created at ~/.wine. After creating a 32-bit Wine prefix and setting the
Windows version to *Windows XP*, you can run your 16-bit and 32-bit Windows
programs with it. For example, to install the BlockBuster Video database:

```
cd ~/WindowsUtils/BlockBuster/   # installation files
WINEARCH=win32 WINEPREFIX="${HOME}/MyWine32Prefix" wine SETUP.EXE
```

After installation, to launch the program:

```
cd ~/MyWine32Prefix/drive_c/Buster2
wine Buster.exe
```

If the software wants the installation CD, set the directory containing the installation
files as a drive with its *Type* (it is hidden) set to *CD-ROM* using `winecfg`.

- **Use `telnet` and `nslookup` to test email servers:** I can build servers from hardware
  to software. After I install the mail server, I need to check if it is configured properly
  and is accessible from outside. Telnet and nslookup are simple but powerful tools
  for this. With `nslookup`, I can find out where the mail server is located for a
  domain.

```
nslookup -query=mx cia.gov
```

This command outputs mail1.cia.gov and mail2.cia.gov as the email servers for the
domain cia.gov. The following telnet transcript shows how I checked if a mailbox (of
the email account) exists on that server and if it accepts incoming email. Today, this
kind of simple testing is possible only in the initial stages of configuring a server.

What is the *CIA rewards program*? In February 2004, the **Central Intelligence Agency
(CIA)** caused worldwide amusement when they published details of their

Iraqi Rewards Program on their website at: http://www.cia.gov/cia/english_rewards.htm

Through this program, the top spying outfit of the U.S. government attempted to solicit intelligence information from the public about "recently-made" Iraqi Weapons of Mass Destruction (WMD). An embarrassed CIA waited for the fuss to die down and covertly removed the English version of the page.

```
$ telnet mail1.cia.gov ██
Trying 1██.██.1██.█...
Connected to mail1.cia.gov.
Escape character is '^]'.
220 mail1b.cia.gov ESMTP
helo helpthecia.com
250 mail1b.cia.gov
mail from: info@helpthecia.com
250 sender <info@helpthecia.com> ok
rcpt to: sh█████@ucia.gov
250 recipient <sh█████@ucia.gov> ok
data
354 go ahead
subject: This is a test
CIA rewards program... is it still on.

.

250 ok:  Message 2█████ accepted
quit
221 mail1b.cia.gov
Connection closed by foreign host.
```

Internet Tasks

- **Download a file no matter what:** I upgraded my Internet connection to a fibre line but it still stalls every now and then. (It seems that some monkeys are playing with the line. The electric supply also get turned off and on multiple times during the day.) So, I have this script to download the most recalcitrant files in the worst of conditions.

```
cd ~/Downloads
wget --continue --tries=100 --wait=20 --no-check-certificate "$1"
```

- **Download online videos**: My internet connection is always bad wherever I live or whichever ISP I use. I am still unable to stream videos. Youtube-DL (or its fork yt-dlp) used to be my solution for downloading videos offline. (I now use a browser script.[86]) Youtube-DL supports several video sites. To download the script, type:

```
wget -c https://yt-dl.org/downloads/latest/youtube-dl
```

Before downloading a video, you need to list the available formats.

```
youtube-dl --list-formats \
          https://www.youtube.com/watch?v=rf4cz_xjgIg
```

The output of this command shows that #22 as the best format. To download the video in this format, try:

```
youtube-dl --format 22 \
          https://www.youtube.com/watch?v=rf4cz_xjgIg
```

Youtube-DL can also convert videos to MP3s if you prefer to download podcast videos.

```
youtube-dl -f 140 -x \
          --audio-format mp3 --audio-quality 96k \
          --exec 'notify-send "Youtube Audio Downloaded" {} ;
                 echo {} > /tmp/ydla-filename.txt' \
          https://www.youtube.com/watch?v=rf4cz_xjgIg
if [ $? -eq 0 ]; then
  nohup ffplay -autoexit -nodisp -hide_banner \
     "$(cat /tmp/ydla-filename.txt)" \
     2> /tmp/ydla-err.log > /tmp/ydla.log &
  # Redirections to prevent littering by nohup

  echo $! > /tmp/ydla-pid.txt
  echo -e "\nTo kill playback midway, type"
  echo 'kill -9 $(cat /tmp/ydla-pid.txt)'
fi
```

- **Test proxies**: Some websites are blocked in India by the government. For some other websites, DDOS-protection services such as CloudFlare block all customers of some Indian ISPs. To access these websites, I need a US-based proxy. There are websites that provide a list of free proxy IPs. Not all of the free proxies function well.

And, not all of them are in the US. An IP by itself does not tell a lot about its location so I have a script that tests the list and reverse lookups the good ones.

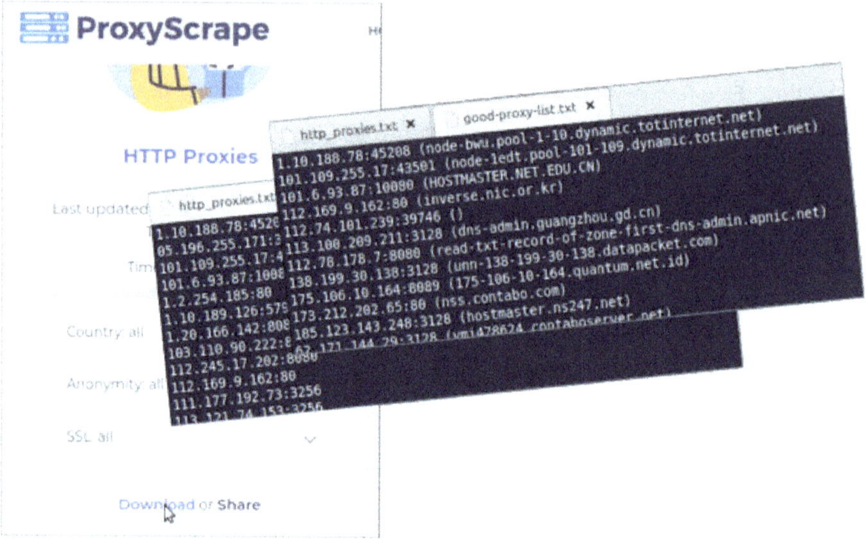

```
cat "${HOME}/Downloads/http_proxies.txt" | sed 's/\r$//' >
"${HOME}/Desktop/http_proxies.txt"
# Convert Windows line endings (\r\n) to Unix ones (\n)

cat "${HOME}/Desktop/http_proxies.txt" | while IFS= read -r sLine
do
  export http_proxy="http://${sLine}"
  # This variable is used by wget as the proxy server

  printf "\nTesting $sLine..."

  wget -q -e use_proxy=yes --spider --timeout=4 --tries=1
http://www.example.com

  if [ $? -eq 0 ]; then
    sIP=$(echo $sLine | awk ' BEGIN { FS=":" } { print $1 }' )
    dig +noall +answer +authority -x $sIP > /tmp/rdnsip.txt

    sRDNS=$(cat /tmp/rdnsip.txt | awk '{ if ($4 == "SOA") { print
$6 }; if ($4 == "PTR") { print $5 }; }')
    printf "\t SUCCESS ($(echo $sRDNS | sed 's/\.$//'))"
    echo "$sLine ($(echo $sRDNS | sed 's/\.$//'))" >>
good-proxy-list.txt
  else
    printf "\t FAIL"
  fi
```

```
done
```

- **Use multiple Firefox profiles:** I have created different Firefox profiles for different kinds of browsing. These profiles are isolated from each other and are stored in separate directories under `~/.mozilla`.

```
# Create a new profile
firefox -ProfileManager
```

When I want to browse behind a US-based proxy IP, I use a special Firefox profile. I create different launchers (shortcuts) on the desktop with the name of their profiles.

```
# Load the profile
firefox -p ProxyIpProfile
```

- **Modify `about:config` settings in Firefox**: These are not command-line tips. If you believe Chrome apologists, only command-line users have the brains to change settings! Type `about:config` in the address box of the Firefox browser. Search for the following settings and change them as described. (Double-clicking will toggle boolean variables.)

  - `browser.tabs.closeWindowWithLastTab`: Set to `false` to prevent a Firefox window from getting closed when the last tab is closed.
  - `dom.event.contextmenu.enabled`: Set to `false` to prevent websites from disabling right click.
  - `dom.event.clipboardevents.enabled`: Set to `false` to prevent websites from contaminating text that you copy from web pages.
  - `media.mediasource.[whatever]`: Set all to `false` to prevent DRM videos from getting loaded and to **download online videos** [86] for offline viewing.
  - `network.trr.mode`: Set to 5 to use your local network's DNS instead of making queries to Cloudfare over https.
  - `app.normandy.enabled`: Set to `false` to disable spyware apps that Mozilla refers to as 'studies'.

Mozilla has been engaged in a relentless struggle to dissuade its thinning band of die-hard followers from using Firefox. Many of the changes are `about:config` are now ineffective. Alternatively, you could create the file `/etc/firefox/policies/policies.json` to trick Firefox into thinking it is in a corporate-controlled computer that is being managed by an administrator rather than the end-user. Here is the `policies.json` that I use.

```
{
  "policies": {
    "Cookies": {
      "ExpireAtSessionEnd": true,
      "Behavior": "reject-foreign",
      "BehaviorPrivateBrowsing": "reject-foreign"
    },
    "DisableAppUpdate": true,
    "DisableBuiltinPDFViewer": true,
```

```json
    "DisableFirefoxStudies": true,
   "FirefoxHome": {
    "Search": false,
    "TopSites": false,
    "Highlights": false,
    "Pocket": false,
    "Snippets": false,
    "Locked": true
   },
   "DisableFirefoxAccounts": true,
   "DisablePocket": true,
   "DisableTelemetry": true,
   "DisplayMenuBar": "always",
   "DNSOverHTTPS": {
    "Enabled":  false
   },
   "DontCheckDefaultBrowser": true,
   "Homepage": {
    "URL": "",
    "Locked": true,
    "StartPage": "none"
   },
   "ManualAppUpdateOnly": true,
   "NetworkPrediction": false,
   "NoDefaultBookmarks": true,
   "OverrideFirstRunPage": "",
   "OverridePostUpdatePage":"",
   "PDFjs": { "Enabled": false },
   "Permissions": {
    "Camera": { "BlockNewRequests": true, "Locked": true },
    "Microphone": { "BlockNewRequests": true, "Locked": true },
    "Location": { "BlockNewRequests": true, "Locked": true },
    "Notifications": { "BlockNewRequests": true, "Locked": true
 },
    "VirtualReality": { "BlockNewRequests": true, "Locked": true
 },
    "Autoplay": { "Default": "block-audio-video", "Locked": true
 }
   },
   "Preferences": {
    "browser.safebrowsing.downloads.enabled": {
     "Value": false,
     "Status": "locked"
    },
```

```json
      "browser.sessionstore.resume_from_crash": {
        "Value": false,
        "Status": "locked"
      },
      "browser.tabs.closeWindowWithLastTab": {
        "Value": false,
        "Status": "locked"
      },
      "dom.event.clipboardevents.enabled": {
        "Value": false,
        "Status": "locked"
      },
      "dom.event.contextmenu.enabled": {
        "Value": false,
        "Status": "locked"
      },
      "browser.search.suggest.enabled": {
        "Value": false,
        "Status": "locked"
      },
      "media.mediasource.enabled": {
        "Value": false,
        "Status": "locked"
      }
    },
    "NewTabPage": false,
    "SanitizeOnShutdown": {
      "Cache": true,
      "Cookies": true,
      "Downloads": true,
      "History": true,
      "Sessions": true,
      "OfflineApps": true
    },
    "SearchBar": "separate",
    "SearchSuggestEnabled": false,
    "UserMessaging": {
      "WhatsNew": false,
      "ExtensionRecommendations": false,
      "FeatureRecommendations": false,
      "UrlbarInterventions": false,
      "SkipOnboarding": false,
      "MoreFromMozilla": false
    }
```

```
    }
  }
```

After creating this file, then create your custom Firefox installations and profiles (using the profile manager commands described earlier). I usually create two Firefox installation with a separate profile for each. One is regularly and manually updated, run without add-ons and used only for secure sites. The other is rarely (or never) updated, contains add-ons and used only for casual read-only browsing.

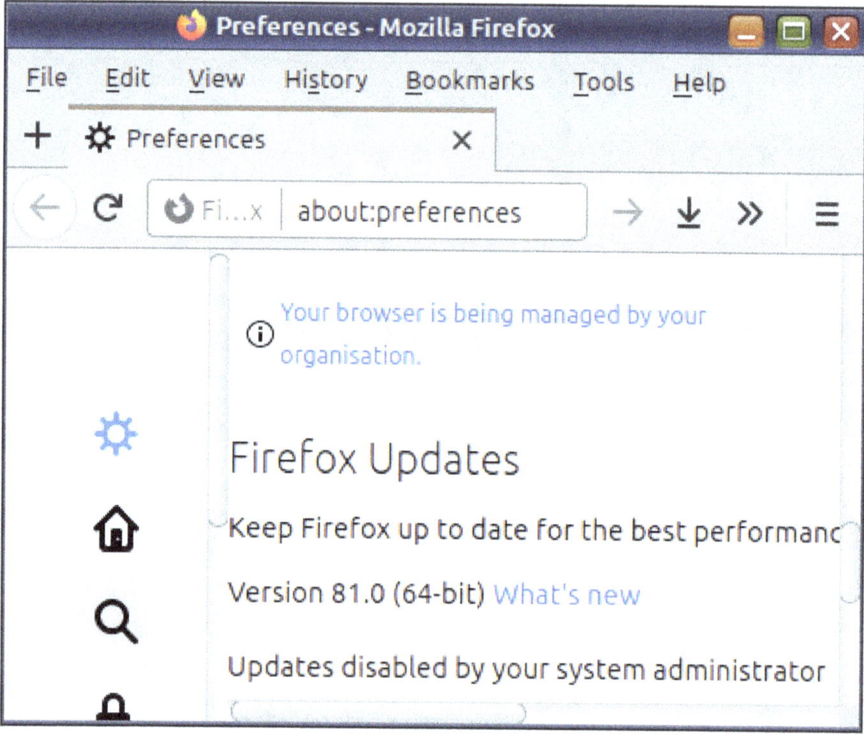

- **Make Seamonkey Mail display dates properly:** Sometimes, you just need the raw date, not yesterday, today or the day before. Create a launcher with this command.

```
export LC_TIME=en_DK.UTF-8 && seamonkey -mail
```

- **Ad-blocker hosts file:** The HOSTS file (`/etc/hosts`) is a remnant from the days when other computers on the network where found using a text file rather than a service like DNS. It is still very useful as an ad-blocker. To block a domain like facebook.com, point it to an non-existent IP address like this:

```
0.0.0.0   facebook.com
```

I have backed up my original hosts as `hosts.original.bak`. There are several sites that provide custom-made hosts file that block adserving and malware-serving sites. I get mine from:

https://github.com/StevenBlack/hosts

One of them was saved as `hosts.blocker.bak` and as `hosts` in the `/etc` directory. I also use a script to append ad-serving domains to the ad-blocking hosts file.

```bash
if [ $# -eq 1 ]; then
  echo 0.0.0.0 $1 >> /etc/hosts.blocker.bak
  cp /etc/hosts.blocker.bak /etc/hosts
else
  echo "No domain specified"
fi
```

When I find a new domain to block, I give the command:

```bash
sudo bash add-to-hosts-file.txt new-offending-domain.com
```

Some websites do not work properly when ads are blocked so I have another script to enable ads.

```bash
cp /etc/hosts.original.bak /etc/hosts
```

- **Use NetCheck:** After years of suffering from poor Internet connectivity, I created a desktop app called **NetCheck** to let me know when the line goes down and comes back up. (I later ported it to Android as well.) The app makes audio and popup notifications but this becomes annoying when the connection is extremely flaky. So, I added options to disable the notifications. The colour of the icon is enough to tell me whether the line is connected or not.

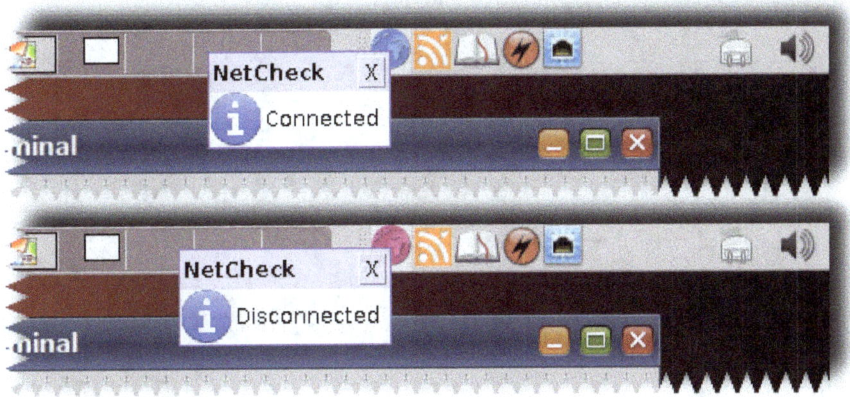


```bash
java -jar netcheck.jar noaudio
java -jar netcheck.jar nopopup
java -jar netcheck.jar noaudio nopopup
```

This app requires the desktop to have a notification applet. Be sure to add it to your desktop before running this command.

- **Check for valid links:** To check whether a link is valid or not, you do not have to download the whole file. Just download the headers. This script makes a HEAD request rather than GET request.

```bash
for sLine in $(< url-list.txt); do
  // Each line contains a URL that needs to be checked
  echo "Checking $sLine"
  sStatus=`curl -s -I $sLine | grep -i "HTTP/[12]"`
  echo -e "\t$sStatus"
```

```bash
    sStatusCode=`echo $sStatus | awk '{ print $2}'`
    if [ "$sStatusCode" -eq "200" ]; then
      echo $sLine >> valid-urls-list.txt
      echo -e "\tValid => \e[33;1m$sLine\e[0m"
    else
      echo $sStatus
      echo -e "\tInvalid => \e[31;1m$sLine\e[0m"
    fi
  done
```

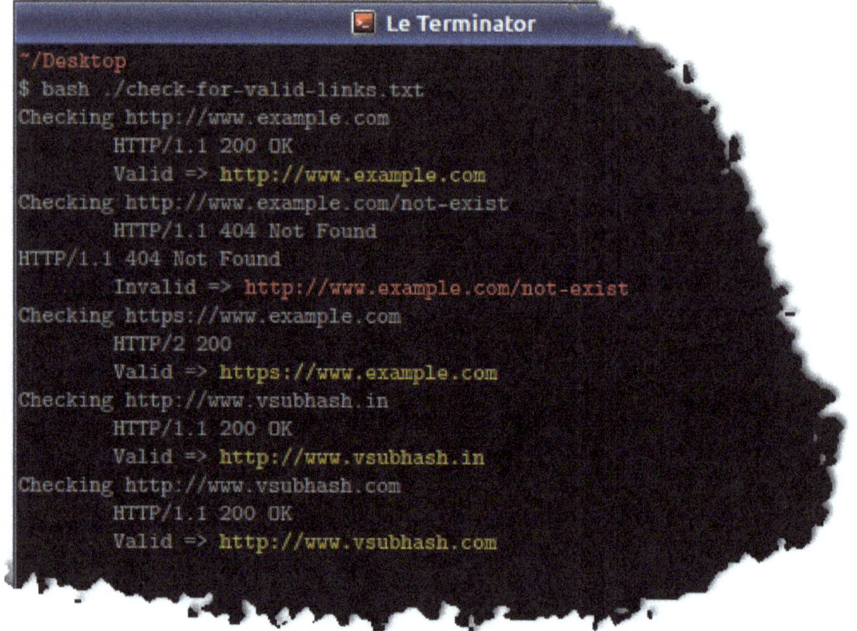

- **More wget tips**:
  - **Backup your WordPress.com blog:** I have two Wordpress blogs. This is how I back them up once a year.

    ```bash
    wget -r \
      --exclude-directories=page,category,author,comments,feed,tag,feed  \
      --mirror --page-requisites \
      --convert-links \
      --span-hosts \
      --domains vsubhash.files.wordpress.com,vsubhash.wordpress.com \
      https://vsubhash.wordpress.com
    ```

  - **Limit the bandwidth:** It is annoying when you start a big download only to find that the rest of browsing has slowed to a crawl. You can allocate how much bandwidth wget can use.

    ```bash
    wget --limit-rate=100k http://www.example.com/download.zip
    ```

- **Disguise `wget`:** So, that uppity website will not talk to crawlers, eh?

```
wget --user-agent='Mozilla/5.0 (Windows NT 10.0; rv:100.0)
Gecko/20100101 Firefox/100.0' \
      http://www.snooty-website.com/download.zip
```

- **Download files of a type listed on a page:** Some pages such as directory listings provide direct links to download files. You need to download files of a particular extension but you do not want to care for the directory structure. Multiple file types can be separated by a comma.

```
# Downloads the audio files but does not create
# any other files or directories
wget -r -accept '*.ogg' --no-directories \
      https://archive.org/download/FibberMcgeeMolly1930s
```

- **Automate FTP tasks:** FTP uses simple text commands, similar to the shell. Software such as FileZilla may let you drag and drop files but internally they use commands such as `ls`, `mv` or `mkdir`. This means that you can automate FTP tasks using scripts containing the necessary FTP commands.

Because it is not good to store a plain text password in an FTP script, you should store it in `base64` encoding. (This can only prevent casual copying.) When you export FTP logins from FileZilla, it will store the passwords in `base64` encoding. You can copy it as is into your FTP upload script. This shell script uses the `lftp` program, instead of the traditional `ftp` program.

```
LUSR="MeUserName"
LPWD=$(echo TWVTZWNyZXRQYXNzd29yZDEyMzQK | base64 --decode)
LPRT="21"
LHOST="ftp.vsubhash.net"


lftp -p ${LPRT} -u ${LUSR},${LPWD} $LHOST << EOF
set ssl:verify-certificate no
cd htdocs
mput screen.png
close
exit
EOF
```

The LPWD variable gets the password (copied from the FileZilla export file) decoded from `base64` encoding. (Because the password can be easily decoded, do not store such scripts online or in insecure locations.) The `lftp` command gets input redirected from a *Here Document*. It begins after one delimiter `EOF` and ends before another delimiter `EOF`. This document contains commands to upload a file to a directory named `htdocs` under the remote root directory. `mput` is the command to upload a local file to that remote directory. (On my server, I turn off the server verification because it uses a temporary SSL certificate. The task is quite a hassle without it.)

- **Check media hype with `curl`:** Some in the Indian financial press suffered a meltdown when it became clear that the foreign import (Chicago Business School's Raghuram Rajan) would not be given a second term as central bank governor. Here is how I assessed the fallout.

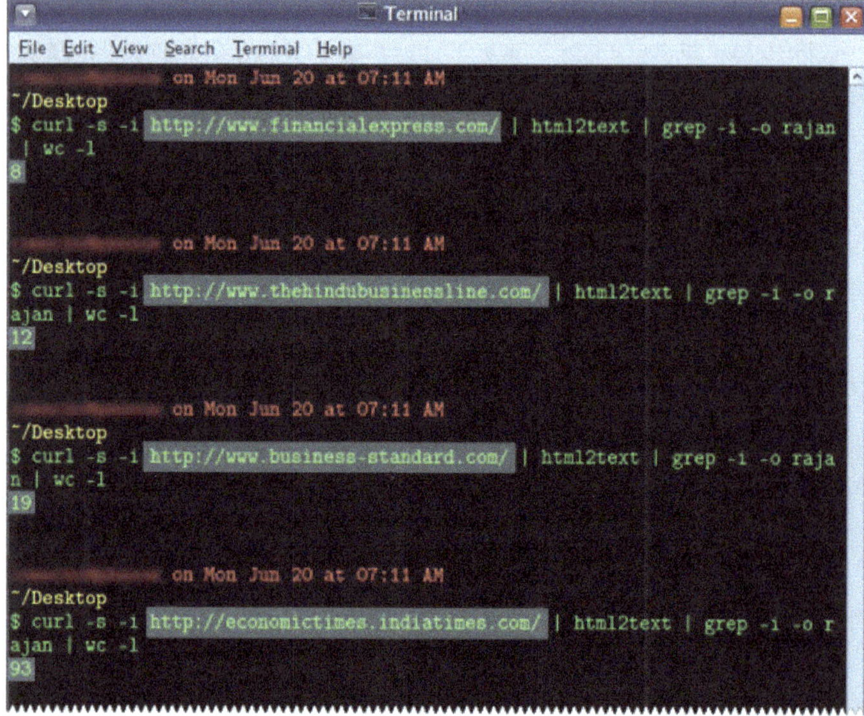

- **Do whois lookups**: The `whois` command requires port 43 to be open.

```
whois example.com | head
```

Multimedia Tasks

- **Run custom commands in image viewers:** Image viewers like Mirage and Pix let you browse images in a folder. Sometimes, you need to run certain commands on a particular image. Mirage refers to such options as 'Custom Actions'. Pix calls them simply as 'Commands'. They have a special notation that you can use to pass values such as the file name or the pathname as parameters to your custom command. The following script will copy the current image's pathname to the clipboard memory.

```
xsel --clear
echo -e "$1\c" | xclip -selection clipboard
notify-send "Image pathname copied" "$1"
```

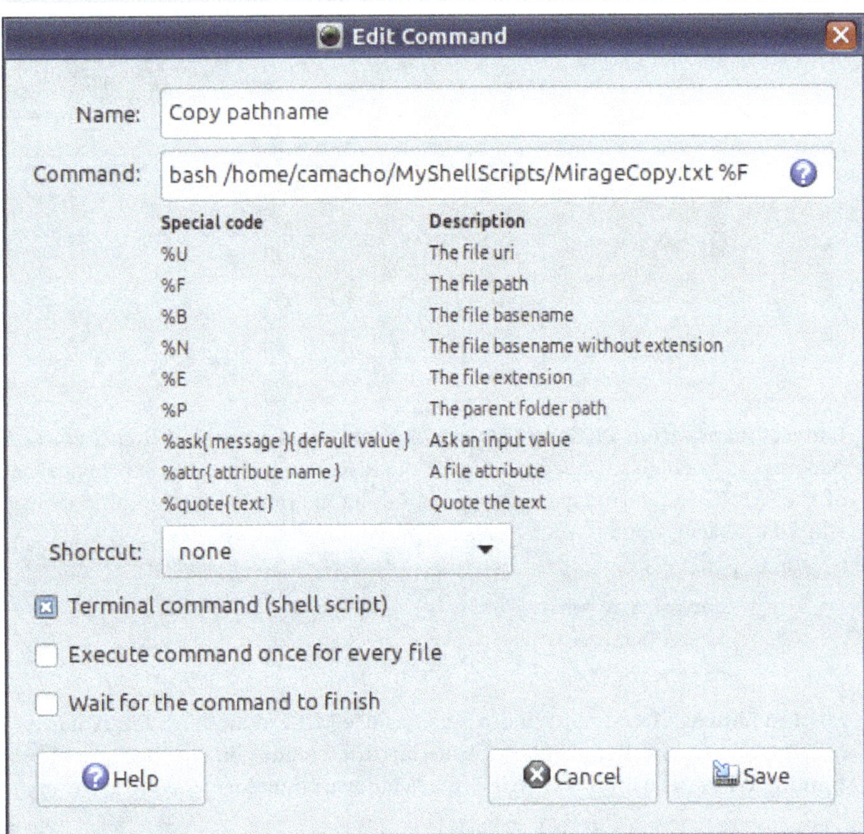

- **Extract GIF frames:** Creating a GIF from several images is *passé*.

```
~/Desktop
$ convert -coalesce ani-linux-usage-among-terrorists-high.gif \
        ani-linux-usage-among-terrorists-high-FRAMES%03d.png


~/Desktop
$ ls ani-*.png
```

```
ani-linux-usage-among-terrorists-high-FRAMES000.png
ani-linux-usage-among-terrorists-high-FRAMES001.png
ani-linux-usage-among-terrorists-high-FRAMES002.png
ani-linux-usage-among-terrorists-high-FRAMES003.png
ani-linux-usage-among-terrorists-high-FRAMES004.png
```

The `-coalesce` switch ensures that you get full frames. (GIF-creation software may crop out transparent regions.) You can peruse this GIF at:

http://www.vsubhash.in/ubuntu-gnome-diary.html

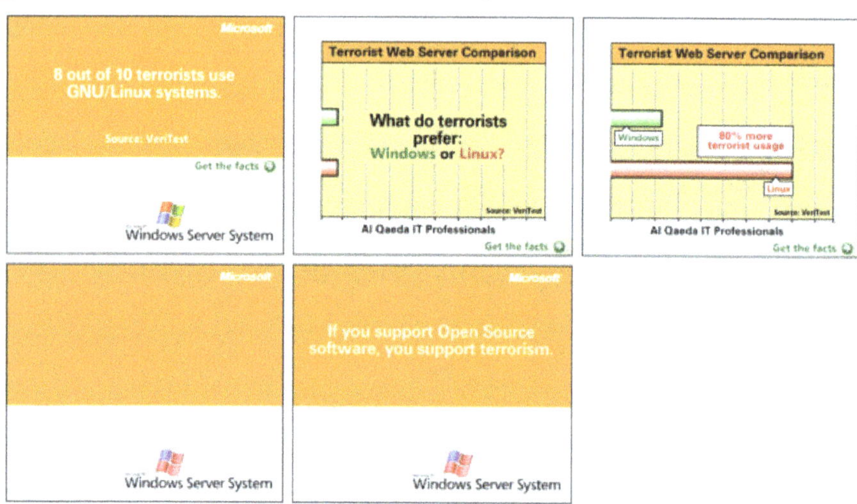

- **Convert transparent PNGs to JPEGs with white background:** When I convert my paperbacks to ebooks, I need to convert the PNG screenshots to JPEG images. Many of these PNGs have transparent regions (alpha channel). Most graphic converters add a dark background to such images. This can be easily avoided.

```
magick screenshot.png \
      -background white \
      -alpha remove \
      screenshot.jpg
```

- **MIDI in Linux:** A lot of old Windows games use MIDI audio files. Linux has its own MIDI synthesizer called Timidity. You can run Timidity in the background when running Windows games with Wine (the Windows emulator).

```
pgrep timidity && pkill timidity
timidity -iA &


cd ~/WinGames/RoadRash
wine -unix ~/WinGames/RoadRash/ROADRASH.EXE
```

- **ASCII art from images**: There are lots of utilities to create ASCII art for words and phrases. More cooler is the conversion of images to ASCII art. For an image with the text "Hello" against a white background, a command such as this:

```
jp2a -f hello.jpg
```

will output:

```
kddOMMMMMOddkWMMMMMMMMMMMMMMMMN:;;kMMO;;;KMMMMMMMMMMMMMM
l;;dMMMMMx;;lWMMMMMMMMMMMMMMMMN:;;kMMO;;;KMMMMMMMMMMMMMM
l;;dMMMMMx;;lMMMMXkolccoxKMMMN:;;kMMO;;;KMMWOxocclxKMM
l;;:lllll:;;lMMWk;;lOKOo;;oWMN:;;kMMO;;;KMWd;;ckOOl;;oW
l;;ckkkkkl;;lMMK;;;clllc;;;OMN:;;kMMO;;;KMK;;;KMMMN:;;O
l;;dMMMMMx;;lMMX:;;dKKKKKKONMN:;;kMMO;;;KMX:;;OMMMK:;;O
l;;dMMMMMx;;lWMMKl:dkkxdloWMN:;;kMMO;;;KMMO:;;odo:;cOM
dllkMMMMMOlldWMMMWOo:;;clxOMMNolloOMMOlllXMMMNkl:;;ckNMM
```

After some filtering with the `tr` command,...

```
jp2a -f hello.jpg | tr 'dkOMNXW' ' '
```

... it output:

```
kddO      Oddk                  :;;k  O;;;
l;;d      x;;l                  :;;k  O;;;
l;;d      x;;l      kolccox     :;;k  O;;;      Oxocclx
l;;:lllll:;;l   k;;lO Oo;;o     :;;k  O;;;      d;;ckOOl;;o
l;;ckkkkkl;;l    ;;;clllc;;;O   :;;k  O;;;      ;;;        :;;O
l;;d      x;;l   :;;d     O     :;;k  O;;;      :;;O       :;;O
l;;d      x;;l   l;:dkkxdlo     :;;k  O;;;      O:;;odo:;cO
dllk      Olld   Oo:;;clxO   ollO   Olll      kl:;:ck
```

The source image was:

- **Disable laptop speaker and enable headphone output:** When you plug in a headphone, the speaker will automatically be muted. If not, the following script will be useful.

```
amixer -c 1 sset 'Master' 80
amixer -c 1 sset 'Speaker' 0
amixer -c 1 sset 'Headphone' 100
```

If set for a launcher, it can mute the speaker with just a click. No need to fiddle with *Sound preferences*.

- **Run Audacious like Winamp:** The audio player Audacious has an alternative interface that looks like classic Winamp. It can even load Winamp skins and presets. I have exported the equalizer presets of Winamp to a file named eq.preset and uploaded it to an online text snippets site. The following commands will download that file and install it to your local Audacious configuration directory.

```
wget -O eq.preset https://pastebin.com/raw/rFmPJapS
mv eq.preset ~/.config/audacious/eq.preset
```

You can copy old Winamp skins to the `/usr/share/audacious/Skins` directory and Audacious will load them too. Another great reason to use Audacious is the support for global hotkeys. By assigning them to function keys, you can control the playback while working on another application.

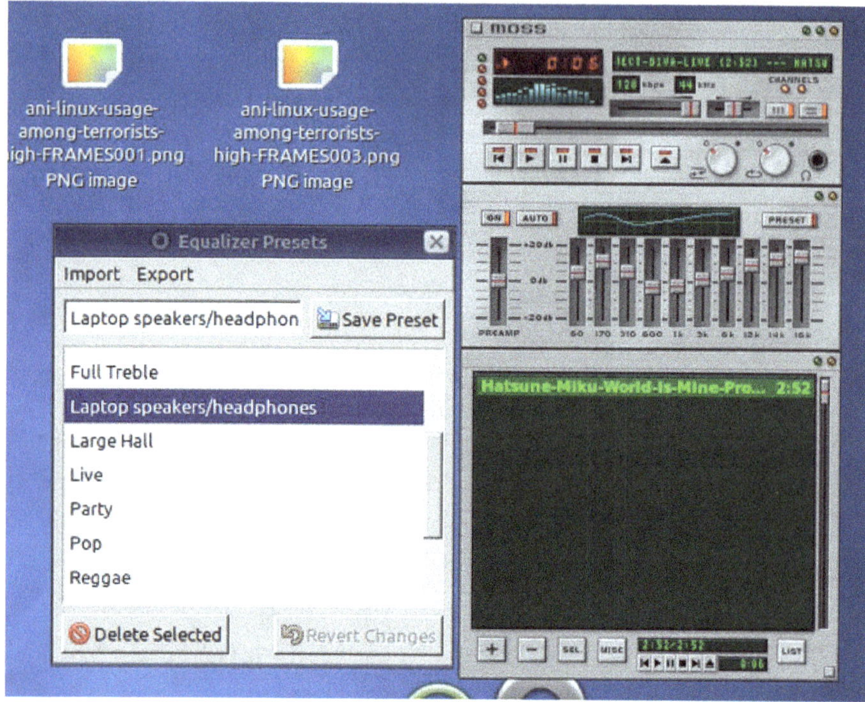

- **FFmpeg:** FFmpeg is a free command-line program for creating, editing, enhancing and converting multimedia files. It supports an unbelievable number of formats and is very easy to use. (I have written an entire book on FFmpeg. Read about it in the backlist.)

  - **Display information about a file:**

    ```
    ffmpeg -i test.mp4
    # or
    ffprobe test.mp4
    ```

  - **Convert from one format to another:**

    ```
    ffmpeg -i video.3gp video.mp4
    ```

  - **Extract audio from a video:**

    ```
    ffmpeg -i video.mp4 -vn video-audio.mp3
    ```

  - **Silence a video:**

    ```
    ffmpeg -i video.mp4 -an video-silent.mp4
    ```

  - **Resize a video:**

    ```
    ffmpeg -i video.mp4 -s vga video-640x480.mp4
    ```

  - **Remove the beginning of a video:**

    ```
    ffmpeg -ss 0:0:20 -i video.mp4 \
    ```

```
            no-titles-video.mp4
```

o **Remove ending of a video:**

```
# Remove last 20 seconds of a 20-minute video
ffmpeg -i video.mp4 \
       -t 0:19:40 \
       no-credits-video.mp4
```

o **Cut from the middle of a video:**

```
# Remove 20 seconds from the beginning
# and ending of a 20-minute video
ffmpeg -ss 0:0:20 -i video.mp4 \
       -t 0:19:40 \
       no-titles-or-credits-video.mp4
```

o **Convert any video to MP4:** When you are archiving videos, you need good compression and good quality. This may not be possible when your videos come from different sources. Here is a Caja Actions Configuration script that will let you optimize your source videos as per your requirements.

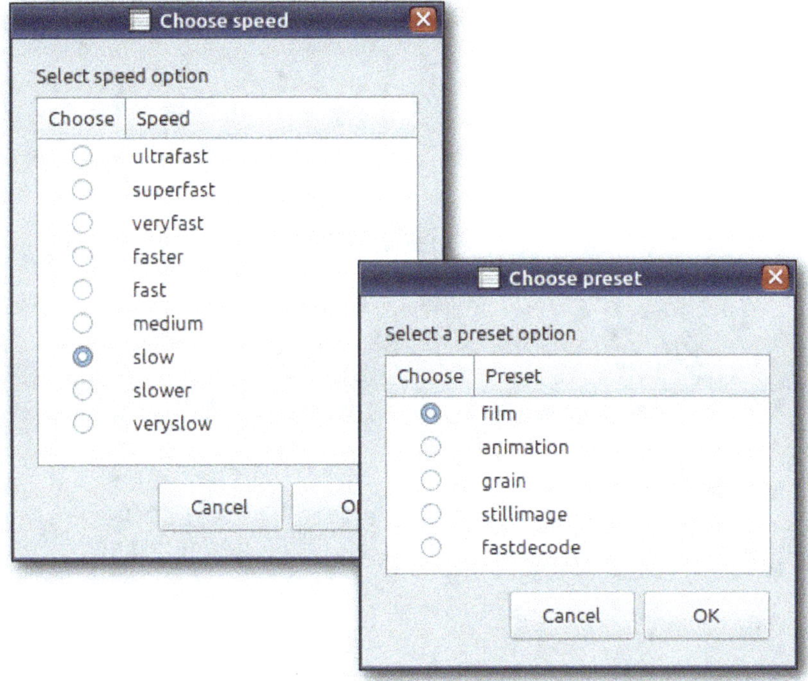


```
# Name:          Convert to MP4
# Description:   Convert this video file to MP4 format
# Command:       terminator
# Parameters:    -x bash Convert-to-MP4.txt %f
# Mimetype:      video/*
```

```bash
# Environment:      Count = 1

sFile="$*"
sFileName=$(basename $sFile)

ffprobe -hide_banner "$sFile"

#read -p "Enter video framerate: " iFrameRate
iFrameRate=24

read -p "Enter video size: " iVideoSize
sPreset=$(zenity --height 300 --title "Choose speed" --text
"Select speed option" --list --radiolist --column "Choose" -
-column "Speed" FALSE 'ultrafast' FALSE 'superfast' FALSE
'veryfast' FALSE 'faster' FALSE 'fast' TRUE 'medium' FALSE
'slow' FALSE 'slower' FALSE 'veryslow')
sTune=$(zenity --title "Choose preset" --text "Select a preset
option" --list --radiolist --column "Choose" --column "Preset"
TRUE film FALSE animation FALSE 'grain' FALSE 'stillimage'
FALSE 'fastdecode')

if [ -z "$sTune" ] || [ -z "$sPreset" ]; then
  exit
fi

sOutputFileName=${sFile%.*}-CONVERTED.mp4
sOutputFile="$sOutputFileName"
echo "Converting to $sOutputFileName"

ffmpeg -y -i "$sFile" \
    -r:v $iFrameRate -s $iVideoSize \
    -filter_complex "setpts=PTS-STARTPTS;
asetpts=N/SAMPLE_RATE/TB" \
    -c:v libx264 -crf 21 -preset "$sPreset" -tune "$sTune"
\
    -c:a aac -b:a 96000 \
    -metadata comment="${sFileName%.*}" \
    "$sOutputFile"

if [ $? -eq 0 ]; then
  notify-send "Success: Conversion to MP4" "$sOutputFileName"
  echo "Success: Conversion to MP4 — $sOutputFileName"
else
  notify-send "Failure: Conversion to MP4" "$sFileName"
  echo "Failure: Conversion to MP4 — $sFileName"
```

- **Extract non-pixellated images from a video:** When a video undergoes lossy compression, there are bound to be artefacts in the video. These become impossible to ignore when you extract still images. You have a better chance at obtaining high-quality stills by limiting yourself to the 'I frames' in the video. I frames or key frames in a video stream have all the data to form a full image.

'P frames' that are immediately before and after an I frame contain data that is limited those regions of the frame that are different from the nearest I frame. When you extract still images, FFmpeg tries to recreate a full frame using data from several frames, not all of them are I frames or key frames. When FFmpeg recreates the frame, it has to do some guess work as the compression is lossy. This results in pixellation, as FFmpeg tries to approximate the data of missing regions.

```
ffmpeg -y -i People-from-Dongbei-are-AWESOME.mp4 \
     -r 1 \
     -f image2 \
     nofilter-still%02d.jpg
```

```
ffmpeg -y -skip_frame nokey \
    -i People-from-Dongbei-are-AWESOME.mp4 \
    -r 1 \
    -f image2 \
    filter-still%02d.jpg
```

The first command above tries to extract frames as usual without any discrimination. The second command picks only I frames. The second command generates several repeats because those I frames are the basis for several intermediary P frames. However, the ones that are found are full-frame images without much pixellation.

If you want a good-quality still from a particular timestamp, try something like this:

```
ffmpeg -y -ss 0:0:20 -skip_frame nokey -i aero-india.mp4 \
    -frames:v 1 -f image2 \
    still20.jpg
```

This command takes a still from the 20-second mark. Do note that when there is a lot of motion in a shot, even an I frame will have artefacts.

- **Convert video to animated GIF:** GIF supports only 256 colours. Still, you can make fun animations with it. However, video-to-GIF conversion is not an exact science. Read more about it from:

  https://engineering.giphy.com/how-to-make-gifs-with-ffmpeg/

  ```
  ffmpeg -y -i baywatch.m4v \
      -filter_complex
      "fps=7,scale=w=320:h=-1:flags=lanczos,split[v1][v2];
      [v1]palettegen=stats_mode=diff[p];
      [v2][p]paletteuse=dither=bayer:bayer_scale=4" \
      run-yasmine-run-4.gif
  ```

  In this software implementation of Chandler Bing's *Run, Yasmine! Run!*, I experimented with the value of the `bayer_scale` filter option.

  - `bayer_scale=0` resulted in discernible pixellation, smoother motion and bigger file size.
  - `bayer_scale=4` resulted in no pixellation, jerky motion and smaller file size.

  Your mileage may vary.

- **Convert video to animated PNG:** A better alternative to GIF animations is APNG. This format has limited support from image-viewing and image-editing applications but has near-universal support from desktop and mobile web browsers. Like PNG and unlike GIF, APNG supports millions of colours. This means that its colours will not have to be downsampled and will be very close to those in the source content. APNG animation files are typically bigger than animated GIFs.

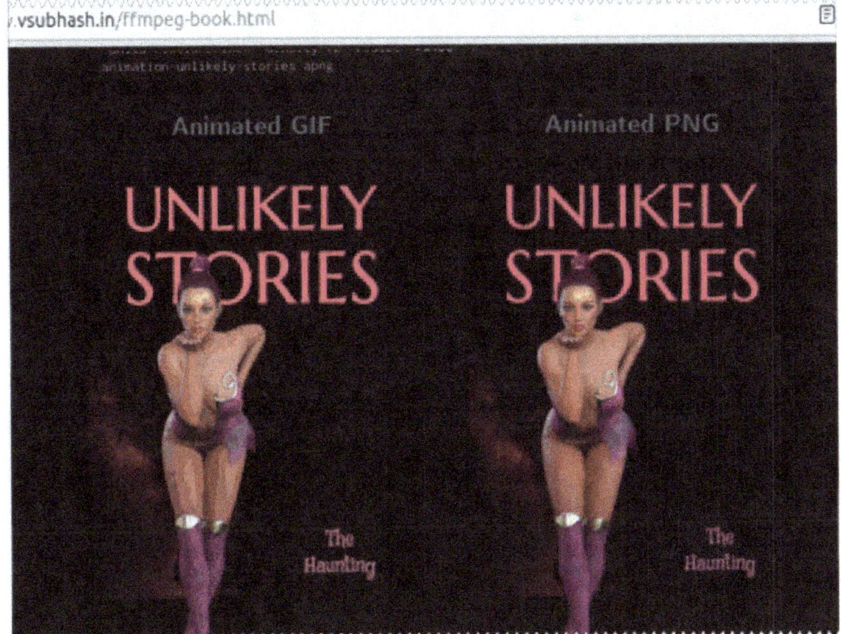

If you are converting GIF animations to APNGs, then ImageMagick is the tool you should use, not `ffmpeg`.

```
magick animated.gif animated.apng
```

The image frames in a GIF will already be downsampled to 256 colours. To create a richer animated PNG, try to use the source frames in PNG format.

```
magick -delay 200 -loop 0 \
       chapter-image-*.png \
       -units PixelsPerInch -density 72 -resize '>x300' \
       animation-unlikely-stories.apng
```

If you are converting a video to APNG, then you can use `ffmpeg`.

```
ffmpeg -i bw.m4v \
       -vf "scale=w=250:h=-2, hqdn3d, fps=6" \
       -dpi 72 -plays 0 \
       bw.apng
```

In this command, `-dpi` is an APNG encoder option and `-plays` is an APNG muxer option. The *high-quality denoise 3d* filter reduces blemishes introduced by the scaling filter. Learn more about these options from the official documentation or by typing:

```
ffmpeg -help muxer=apng
ffmpeg -help encoder=png
ffmpeg -help filter=hqdn3d
```

- **Letterbox any video:** Because of connectivity problems, I am not able to stream online videos. Instead, I mass-download them and see them offline. My new but cheap TV is unable to play hi-resolution videos. I use this script to quickly downsample the downloaded videos. Quality is not important as these are mostly informative talking-head videos.

```
# Quickly reduce any video to 640x360 (nhd)
sFile="$*"
sOutputFile=${sFile%.*}-letterboxed.mp4
ffmpeg -y -i "$sFile" \
        -vf "scale=size=nhd:
            force_original_aspect_ratio=decrease:
            force_divisible_by=2,
            pad=w=640:h=360:x=(ow-iw)/2:y=(oh-ih)/2:
            color=black" \
        -crf 31 -preset ultrafast -r 24 -c:a copy \
        "$sOutputFile"
```

- **Create a meme video:** The following command renders some text and a video segment on a green background.

```
ffmpeg -y -i Prime-Time.mp4 \
        -ss 0:43:51 -t 0:0:33 \
        -filter_complex "color=c=green:s=640x360[c];

[c]drawtext=x=20:y=20:fontcolor=yellow:alpha=0.6:shadowx=1:shad
owy=1:textfile=t1.txt:fontsize=22:fontfile=/usr/share/fonts/tru
etype/Dummies_.ttf[t1];
```

```
[t1]drawtext=x=270:y=320:fontcolor=yellow:alpha=0.6:shadowx=1:s
hadowy=1:textfile=t2.txt:fontsize=22:fontfile=/usr/share/fonts/
truetype/Dummies_.ttf[t2];

[t2]drawtext=x=10:y=330:fontcolor=white:alpha=0.6:textfile=t3.t
xt:fontsize=16:fontfile=/usr/share/fonts/truetype/SourceSerifPr
o-It.ttf[t3];
                        [0:v:0]crop=640:250:0:35[v];
                        [t3][v]overlay=0:55" \

        aoc-faa.mp4
```

There is no need to spend huge sums of money on proprietary software when FFmpeg can do it for free. This video composition used multiple videos, images, text and fonts. (The deep fakery was done by somebody else.)

This video was also output as a looping animated GIF. Learn how it was created from:

> http://www.vsubhash.in/blogs/blog/2022-10-02-video-composting-using-ffmpeg.html

I have created several such videos using FFmpeg for my FFmpeg book. These videos are available in a playlist at:

> http://www.vsubhash.in/ffmpeg-book.html

- **Play videos with `ffplay`**: I do not stream online video channels. I mass-download the videos and see them offline. One common problem with many of these videos is low volume. They are caused by high-volume spikes caused by loud intro/outro sequences or unintentional shakes to the microphone. Another problem is inadequate contrast caused by excessive lighting, light-coloured backgrounds or just bad colour settings in the camera or video-editing software. On my computer, I use `ffplay` as the media player and I use its filters to correct these problems.

```
sFile="$*"
sTitle=$(basename "${sFile}")
iDur=$(ffprobe -select_streams v:0  \
        -show_entries "stream=duration" \
        -print_format "default=nokey=1:noprint_wrappers=1" \
```

```bash
        -i "${sFile}" 2> /dev/null)

if [ "$iDur" = "N/A" ]; then
  notify-send "FFplay compressor" "Duration stream information
not found"
  exit
fi


ffplay \
  -x 600 -y 337 -left 200 -top 200 -hide_banner -autoexit \
  -window_title "$sTitle" \
  -vf "eq=saturation=1.6,
   drawtext=x=round(W*t/${iDur}):y=H-th-1:
     fontfile='${HOME}/.fonts/Inter-Regular.ttf':
     fontsize=round(H/20):fontcolor=FFAABBDD:
     text='□',
   drawtext=x=W-tw-20:y=H-th-20:
     fontfile='${HOME}/.fonts/Time-Normal.ttf':
     fontsize=round(H/30):fontcolor=FFFFFF77:
     text='%{eif\:mod(t/3600\,60)\:d\:2}\:%
{eif\:mod(t/60\,60)\:d\:2}\:%{eif\:mod(t\,60)\:d\:2}'" \
  -af "dynaudnorm=gausssize=3" \
  "$sFile"
```

The filters increase colour contrast and forcibly normalizes the video. (This is
okay for amateur videos but not recommended for movies or music videos.)
There is also a progress slider on the bottom edge and a timer in the bottom-right
corner. More info on this tip is available at:

http://www.vsubhash.in/blogs/blog/2023-12-23-how-to-play-videos-using-
ffmpeg-s-own-media-player-ffplay.html

Office Tasks

- **Use a text browser**: Lynx is a lightweight text-only Web browser. When you copy text from it, it copies plain text. You can paste the text into a LibreOffice document without all the rich-text formatting that a regular browser might copy.

- **Calender:** I discovered this `cal` command recently. There is no need to leave the console and click the system tray to check the calendar.

- **Use MarkDown for text documents:** If you write a lot of text for use on the Web or in documents such as DOCX, ODT or PDF, then it is best if you write it in plain text. Or, rather in *MarkDown*. MarkDown is an easy human-readable text format that can serve as the common base for exporting to multiple document formats such as HTML, ODF, DOC/DOCX, PDF and ebook (EPUB, MOBI...). It is a great tool for authors, technical writers and content developers to create books, manuals, web pages and other rich-text content. **CommonMark** is its new standardized avatar (www.CommonMark.org). I wrote the first book on the subject — *CommonMark Ready Reference*.

(All my books [94] including this one were written in CommonMark.) The original MarkDown executable was a Perl script. CommonMark is available as a binary executable written in C and is blazingly fast. You can download it (Linux/Windows) from my website at:

http://www.vsubhash.in/commonmark.html

You can convert your CommonMark/MarkDown files like this:

```
cmark --unsafe --validate-utf8 sample.txt.md > sample.htm
```

- **Convert text to HTML with Unicode encoding:** When you convert MarkDown to HTML, the HTML will not have `<head>` or `<body>` tags. If you load the output HTML files in a browser, it will most likely be displayed with the wrong encoding. A word such as 'dæmon' may be displayed as 'dÃ¦mon'. To ensure such things do not happen, wrap the HTML with the appropriate tags.

```
sHtmlFile="${1%.*}.htm"


echo "<!DOCTYPE html>" > $sHtmlFile
echo "<head><meta http-equiv=\"Content-Type\" content=\"text/html;
charset=UTF-8\" /></head><body>" >> $sHtmlFile


cmark --unsafe --validate-utf8  "$1" >> $sHtmlFile


echo "</body></html>" >> $sHtmlFile
```

Browsers will now be able to display this HTML with the proper encoding. However, it will be using the built-in basic CSS stylesheet used by the browser. If you customize the template with your own CSS and Javascript, you can do wonders with it. This book would not have looked so well formatted without my custom CSS and Javascript.

- **Detect non-existent images in a HTML page**: The PDF creation process for my books is automated. The ebook creation is not entirely automated. When I add a PNG image to the paperback, I might forget to include its JPEG version in the ebook directory. To detect such images, I open the ebook's HTML fie in Firefox browser and then in the Web console (Developer Tools), I type the following:

```javascript
document.querySelectorAll("body img").forEach((el, ind , arr) =>
{
  if (arr[ind].naturalHeight == 0) {
    console.error(arr[ind].src + " not loaded");
  } else {
    console.log(" ——— " + arr[ind].src+ " ——— ");
  }
});
```

This code will show error messages for any unloaded images.

- **Convert HTML to ODT, DOCX and PDF:** LibreOffice (the free alternative to Microsoft Office) has a headless operation mode. If you have a valid HTML document without any dynamic content (loaded by Javascript), then you can convert it to a LibreOffice ODT file. It is best if you have created the HTML from a MarkDown file as described in the previous tip.

```bash
# Creates document.odt
libreoffice --convert-to "odt" document.html


# Creates document.docx
libreoffice --convert-to "docx" document.odt


# Creates document.pdf
libreoffice --convert-to "pdf" document.odt
```

If the document refers to local images, then they will not be available in the ODT, DOCX or PDF. You need encode the images within the HTML (`base64` encoding) in the SRC attribute of the `img` HTML tags. Modify the first statement to include the HTML filter `HTML:EmbedImages`.

```bash
# Creates document.html (with text-encoded images)
# inside some-other-directory
libreoffice --convert-to "html:HTML:EmbedImages" \
            --outdir some-other-directory \
            document.html
```

When you convert this HTML to ODT or DOCX in this way, the documents will be fully self-contained and not be dependent on external image files. However, any sophisticated formatting that you have added using custom CSS or Javascript will be lost. If you want to convert a HTML to PDF without losing the formatting, then use `wkhtmltopdf`. This tool uses a headless Firefox browser and then prints the CSS-styled HTML content to PDF. I create print-ready PDFs of my book manuscripts (written in CommonMark) using this utility.

- **Convert HTML to MarkDown:** Firefox does a better job of converting HTML to text (almost MarkDown) but this command will do for simple HTML files.

  ```
  html2text sample.htm > sample.md.txt
  ```

- **Convert PDF to images:** There are several utilities for this task.

  ```
  # Export pages 2-20 of the PDF to JPEG at 120 dpi
  # with 'animalia-page' prefix

  pdftoppm -jpeg -jpegopt quality=94 \
          -r 120 \
          -f 2 -l 20 \
          "animalia-humorosum.pdf" \
          animalia-page
  ```

- **Convert images to PDF:** ImageMagick (formerly known as `convert`) can be used for this task.

  ```
  # Export pages numbered 1 and 12 as a two-page PDF
  magick -units PixelsPerInch \
          -density 144x144 \
          page-01.jpg -resize 100% \
          page-12.jpg -resize 100% \
          delinearized.pdf
  ```

- **Print to PDF:** Some application do not print to PDF. They generate a PostScript file with a '.ps' extension. You can use the `ps2pdf` utility to convert the PostScript file to PDF.

  ```
  ps2pdf test.ps test.pdf
  ```

- **Combine PDFs:** The first page of this book is based on its cover. I used ImageMagick to export it to a PDF. The rest of the pages were exported from CommonMark as a second PDF. I need to combine them before I send it to the printers. How do I do it?

  ```
  pdftk cat first-page.pdf interior-pages.pdf output book.pdf
  ```

- **Decrypt PDF:** If you pass the password in the command-line, it will get recorded in the history file. (If you start the command with a space, it will not.) I use this script with the pathname of an encrypted PDF to decrypt it. The prompt for the password does not get echoed on the screen.

  ```
  stty -echo
  read -p "Type the password: " sPassword
  stty echo

  # You can also use the built-in -s switch of read
  # read -sp "Type the password: " sPassword
  ```

```bash
# Alternatively you can get the password using a GUI widget
# sPassword=$(zenity --password --title "Decrypt PDF" --text "Type
the password")

qpdf --password=$sPassword \
    --decrypt "$1" \
    "${1%.*}-unencrypted.pdf"
```

You can encrypt a PDF with a similar script, as listed in a previous chapter. [36]

- **Convert PDF to DjVu:** Archive.org has a lot of books as scanned PDFs. The pages are high-quality images and open very slowly on phones and tablets. You can convert such PDFs to the DjVu format for more responsiveness on such devices.

  ```bash
  pdf2djvu -o "$1" "${1%.*}.djvu"
  ```

- **Display image pixel density**: ImageMagick provides a handful of programs to perform different types of action. One of them is `identify`. It is used to retrieve image information. To display the pixel density, you can try:

  ```bash
  identify -units PixelsPerInch -format '%x×%y' image.png
  ```

  When building my PDF books, I need to check if all images are at 300 dpi. To check this, I use:

  ```bash
  # Display DPI (resolution)
  for sFile in *.jpg *.png; do
    echo -e "$sFile\t$(identify -units PixelsPerInch \
                                 -format '%x × %y' $sFile)"
  done
  ```

- **Display image dimensions**: When building my ebooks, I need to ensure that images are not too big. Ebook readers do not do a good job of scaling images. The images need to be just right.

  ```bash
  for sFile in *.jpg; do
    echo -e "$sFile\n\t$(identify -units PixelsPerInch \
                                  -format '%w × %h @ %x dpi' \
  $sFile)"
  done
  ```

- **Set pixel density of an image** : Ideally, an image should be saved with enough pixels required by its DPI. A lot of photographs are saved with 72 dpi. For printing, a DPI is 300 is considered minimum. You will have to downsize it or scale it down and then save it at 300 dpi. This is not a problem because most cameras and phones take very images that are several times bigger than printed pages. Downscaling will ensure that the image has adequate number of pixels at the higher DPI.

  Sometimes, the image is already small and at 72 dpi. Scaling it down further is not an option. To ensure that the printing process/application does not downsize the image, you need to manually set the DPI at 300. This can be done using `magick`.

  ```bash
  magick "$sFile" -units PixelsPerInch -density 300 small-image.png
  ```

Such images may not get downsized but can become over-pixellated.

To set the DPI *en masse*, use:

```
# Set paperback DPI
for sFile in *.jpg *.png; do
  magick "$sFile" -units PixelsPerInch -density 300 \
         "another_directory/${sFile}"
done
```

- **Check embedded colour profiles in an image**: You can use `identify` for this too.

  ```
  identify -format '%[profiles]' image.png
  ```

  When I convert my HTML files to PDF, `khtmltopdf` throws a warning whenever it finds an image with an embedded colour profile. I use this code to find them.

  ```
  # Display profiles
  for sFile in *; do
    echo -e "$sFile\t$(identify -format '%[profiles]' $sFile)"
  done
  ```

- **Export image to PDF in CMYK colourspace**: For my book covers, I need to create a PDF with the cover image saved using the print-standard *CMYK* colour profile. I develop my cover images in GIMP, which does not support CMYK. When I convert a cover image to PDF, it is saved with sRGB colorspace. This results in a slight difference in the colors when the cover are printed. To avoid that, I can use a CMYK colour profile.

  ```
  magick book-cover.png -profile
         "/usr/share/color/icc/ghostscript/default_cmyk.icc" \
         -colorspace CMYK book-cover.pdf
  ```

The colours in a CMYK PDF may look somewhat different from those in the image file. This is expected. The colours of images displayed on a screen are **emitted** from the pixels. The colours of the print copy (the PDF) are reflected of a white cover. Its *subtractive* colours are going to be different. You can check if the CMYK PDF is accurate using `pdftoppm`. [If you had used the `-jpeg` or `-png` option, images created from a CMYK PDF will also look somewhat washed out.]

```
pdftoppm -jpegcmyk -r 300 book-cover.pdf covers
```

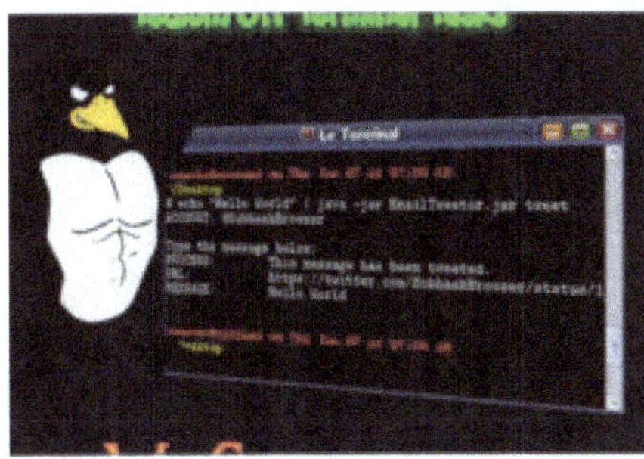
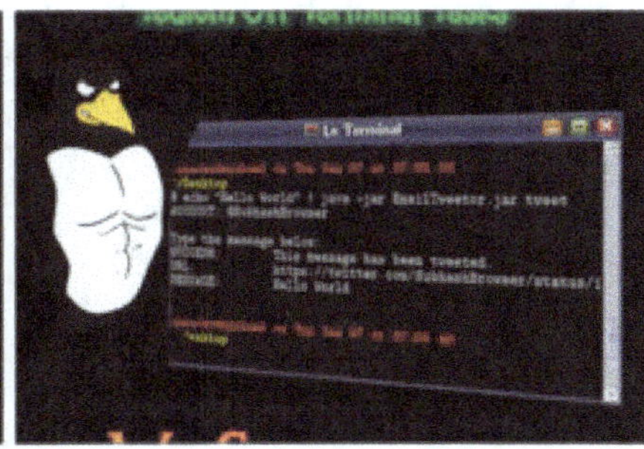

What the specific printer chooses to do may be another matter. The `identify` program finds old Amazon cover templates as CMYK and new ones as sRGB. Their online images of the cover have always looked different from what you upload. With CMYK PDFs, online book thumbnails can look worse. When buying books online, most people judge books by the cover. A lot of printers will automatically convert sRGB PDFs to CMYK. Some slight colour differences in the printed cover should not be a problem.

```
magick book-cover.png \
        -profile "sRGB-IEC61966-2-1.icc" \
        book-cover.pdf
```

The .icc file is a colour profile I was able to save from GIMP when I opened the Amazon cover template.

- **Remove embedded colour profiles**: For this, we need to use `magick`.

```
magick "$sFile" +profile "*" image.png
```

The option `-profile` is used to add a profile. The option `+profile` is used to remove a profile. The value `"*"` ensures that all profiles are removed.

In a directory full of images, I can do:

```
# Remove ICC profiles
for sFile in *.png *.jpg; do
  magick "$sFile" +profile "*" "another_directory/${sFile}"
done
```

When you remove all colour profile, the screen-standard *sRGB* colour profile is assumed.

- **Scale down only big images**: Sometimes, you need to scale images only when the dimensions are above or below a threshold. In this code snippet, the option value 600> ensures that only images wider than 600 pixels are resizes. The option value part x600 does the same for the height.

```
for sFile in *.png *.jpg; do
  if [ -f "../../html/images/${sFile%.*}.png" ]; then
    magick "../../html/images/${sFile}" \
            -units PixelsPerInch -density 96 -resize '600>x600>' \
            -background white -alpha remove \
            +profile "*" \
            "${HOME}/Desktop/FasDrive/${sFile%.*}.jpg"
  else
      magick "../../html/images/${sFile}" \
          -units PixelsPerInch -density 96 -resize '600>x600>' \
          +profile "*" \
          "${HOME}/Desktop/FasDrive/${sFile%.*}.jpg"
  fi
done
```

I use this code snippet to downscale and convert high-resolution images of my paperback PDFs for the ePUB ebook. EPUB ebooks require only JPEG images and the images do not have to be high-resolution. The command also removes any non-SRGB colour profiles.

- **Set image quality**: When you are converting to JPEG or PNG format, remember to set `-quality` option. You do not want the file size to increase when you are downsizing an image. It happens. The range for this option is from 1 (least) to 100 (best). For the lossless PNG format, use 100 for maximum (but slow) compression. For the lossy JPEG format, I use 94 for good quality and adequate compression. (A value of 80 is usually enough.) For an existing JPEG image, query the current quality (using `identify`) and use that value. I automate such operations using a Caja Action. [32]

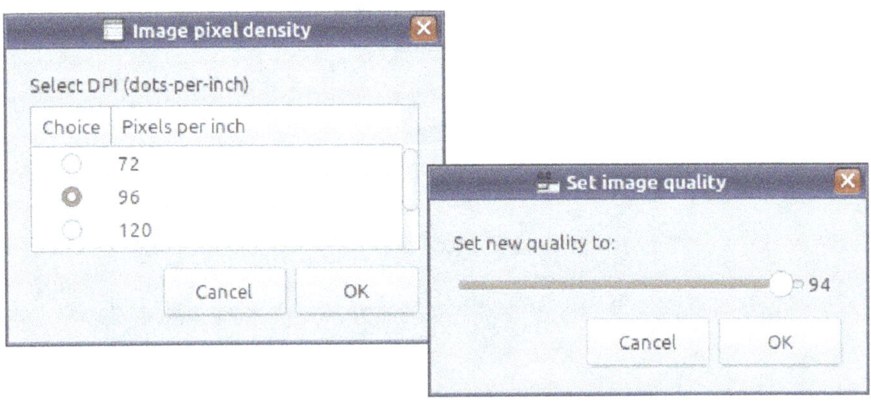

```
sImageBackup="/tmp/${sFileName}.bak.${sFileExt}"
cp "$*" "${sImageBackup}"
# $* is the currently selected image file


iDensity=$(zenity --title "Image pixel density" \
                  --text "Select DPI (dot-per-inch)" \
                  --list --radiolist \
                  --column "Density" \
                  --column "Pixels per inch" \
       FALSE '72' \
       TRUE '96'  \
       FALSE '120' \
       FALSE '150' \
       FALSE '300' \
       FALSE '600' )

...

iExistingQuality=$(identify -format '%Q' "${sImageBackup}")
iQuality=$(zenity --scale --title="Set image quality" \
                  --text="Set new quality to: " \
                  --min-value=1 --max-value=100 \
```

```
                    --value=${iExistingQuality} --step=1)

magick "${sImageBackup}" -quality ${iQuality} \
       -units PixelsPerInch -density $iDensity \
       "$*"
```

- **Grab a screenshot of a web page**: Firefox can take screenshots of web pages. You need to close all open windows of Firefox before trying this command.

  ```
  firefox --screenshot vsubhash-com.png http://www.vsubhash.com
  ```

  This command may fail if Firefox is unable to become headless. If you log in to another user account [39] and then try the command, Firefox will be forced to run headless and be able to take the screenshot.

Miscellaneous Tips & Tricks

In this chapter, I have included tips and tricks not necessarily related to the command-line. Consider it as a bonus.

- **Compose key:** In Microsoft Windows, if you wanted to type the copyright (©) symbol, you had to hold down the [ALT] key and type 0169 on the numeric keypad. You cannot do the same in Linux. Linux users need to first designate a modifier key in the keyboard as the *Compose* key. I suggest you select the useless left Windows key for it. (From the Mate desktop menu, select **Preferences » Keyboard » Layouts » Options » Compose key position » Left Win**).

To type the copyright symbol, press these keys in a sequence:

- Compose and 0 — Hold down the Compose key and then press the O key once.

- C — Release the Compose key and press the C key once.

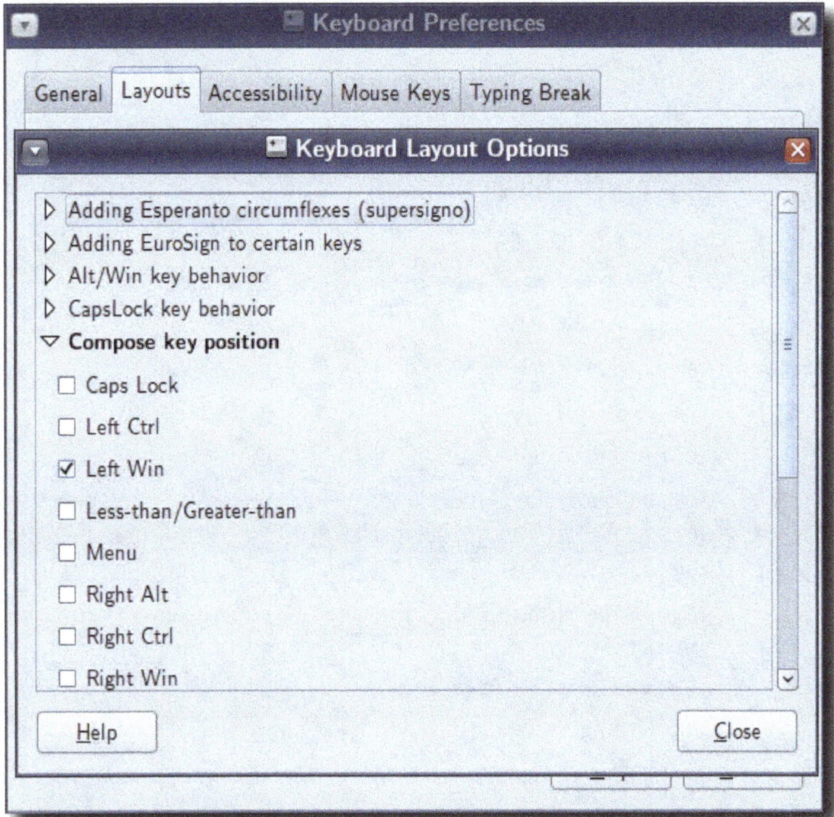

This table lists several symbols that you can type using the Compose key (printed as ▣):

Key	Description	First	Second
©	Copyright	▣ and o	c

Symbol	Description	Key combination	
®	Registered	▤ and o	r
™	Trademark	▤ and t	m
€	Euro	▤ and =	e
£	Sterling pound	▤ and =	l
¥	Japanese Yen	▤ and -	y
á	'a with accent' as in *á la*	▤ and '	a
è	'e with grave' as in *cafè*	▤ and `	e
ā	'a with macron' as in *Vāstu Shāstrā*	▤ and -	a
ö	'o with diaeresis or umlaut' as in *Österreich*	▤ and " (SHIFT, ▤ and ')	o
ê	'e with circumflex' as in *fête*	▤ and ^ (SHIFT, ▤ and 6)	o
ç	'c with cedilla' as in *française*	▤ and ,	c
ñ	'n with tilde' as in *El Niño*	▤ and ~ (SHIFT, ▤ and `)	n
æ	'a with e' as in *Cæsar*	▤ and a	e
œ	'a with e' as in *amœba*	▤ and o	e
ø	'o with stroke' as in *østersøø*	▤ and /	o
ß	'sharp s' as in *straße*	▤ and s	s
§	section	▤ and s	o
¶	para	▤ and !	p
'	opening quotation mark	▤ and <	'
'	closing quotation mark	▤ and >	'
"	opening double quotation mark	▤ and <	"
"	closing double quotation mark	▤ and >	"
«	opening quotation chevron	▤ and <	<
»	closing angle quotation chevron	▤ and >	>
→	right arrow	▤ and -	>
←	left arrow	▤ and <	-
µ	micro	▤ and /	u
·	middot	▤ and ^	.
…	ellipsis	▤ and .	.
°	degree	▤ and o	o

Character	Description	Compose keys	
°	non-breaking space	⌨ and ⎵	⎵
1	superscript 1	⌨ and s	1
2	superscript 2	⌨ and s	2
÷	division	⌨ and -	+
×	multiplication	⌨ and x	x
±	plus or minus	⌨ and +	-
½	half	⌨ and 1	2
⅙	one-sixth	⌨ and 1	6
☺	smiley face	⌨ and :	)
☹	frowning face	⌨ and :	(

If a keypress requires the use of a Shift key, press and hold the Shift key and then press and hold the Compose key.

Some characters such as '—' (em dash)(⌨, -, - and -), '–' (en dash) (⌨, -, - and .) and ② (circled number 2) (⌨, (, 2 and)) require a third keypress.

If the Compose key times out before you can press the second key, adjust the *Repeat Keys* timings (from the desktop menu, select *System » Preferences » Hardware » Keyboard » Keyboard Preferences*). Better take some screenshots before messing up with those settings.

- **Typing by Unicode value:** To type by Unicode, you need to first hold CTRL + SHIFT and then press the 'u' key once. You will then see a underlined 'u' character waiting for you to type a Unicode number. Release Ctrl and Shift keys. Type the number and press the Enter key. The underline 'u' character will be replaced by the type number's Unicode character.

  For example, the Unicode value for the tab-length whitespace character is 2007. To type the character, you may have to

  - hold down CTRL + SHIFT and press u once
  - release the CTRL + SHIFT
  - type 2, 0, 0, 7 and press ENTER.

  If after pressing CTRL + SHIFT + u, you decide not to type any Unicode codepoint, you can of course press ESC.

  For the non-breaking hyphen (-), the Unicode value is 2011. For non-breaking narrow space, it is 202F. For the Indian rupee symbol (₹), the Unicode value is 20B9.

  Consult the *Character Map* utility (use its search function) to know the Unicode values of different characters.

- **Rupee symbol:** The Indian rupee has a currency symbol in the Unicode table. If you change the keyboard to *India with Rupee sign*, you can press right ALT key followed by the 4 key to type the ₹ symbol.

- **Type Unicode flag symbols:** Between 1F1E6 and 1F1FF, Unicode has special alphabets from A to Z. What is special about them? These codepoints are for displaying the flag symbols of several countries. First, you need to identify the ISO country code for a country. For India, it is IN. For the USA, it is US. For Russia, it is RU. As mentioned above, you need to hold down `CTRL` + `SHIFT` and then press the 'u' key. Then, you type to Unicode code point for the individual letter in the country code. Finally, you press `ENTER`. When you type `I` and `N` country codes one after another, they transform into the Indian flag.

Flag / Letter	Code	Letter	Code
🇮🇳	u1F1EE + u1F1F3	K	1F1F0
🇺🇸	u1F1FA + u1F1F8	L	1F1F1
🇷🇺	u1F1F7 + u1F1FA	M	1F1F2
		N	1F1F3
A	1F1E6	O	1F1F4
B	1F1E7	P	1F1F5
C	1F1E8	Q	1F1F6
D	1F1E9	R	1F1F7
E	1F1EA	S	1F1F8
F	1F1EB	T	1F1F9
G	1F1EC	U	1F1FA
H	1F1ED	V	1F1FB
I	1F1EE	W	1F1FC
J	1F1EF	X	1F1FD
		Y	1F1FE
		Z	1F1FF

- **Launch a file in its default GUI application** : `xdg-open` can be used to open a file in its default *windowy* viewer or editor.

```
### Displays image in the default image viewer
xdg-open Screenshot.png
```

```
### Edits document in LibreOffice Writer
xdg-open Untitled.odt
```

- **Move processes to a different core:** All PCs sold today have multicore CPUs. However, you will find that most process are loaded on to the first core. The other cores see less action. You can remedy this by setting the core affinity of some programs.

```
# Move the process to the second core
taskset -c 1 firefox
```

- **Use Seamonkey:** I do not do any financial transactions on mobile devices. I use a desktop for them. Even then, I do not use Firefox. I use Seamonkey. Many decades ago, Netscape had an 'Internet Communication Suite' that combined several Internet apps including a browser, email client, chat client, and addressbook. Today, the Seamonkey project has followed its footsteps with an all-in-one suite combining Firefox, Thunderbird and ChatZilla. I use Seamonkey exclusively for financial transactions and email. Firefox can go to risky websites but Seamonkey? Never! Isolation is the key to security.

- **GreaseMonkey scripts:** You can extend or modify the functionality of websites in your browser using *user scripts*. I have GreaseMonkey scripts that will parse a Facebook timeline or a Twitter feed and delete every post, one by one. You can find many of them at:

User scripts are Javascript scripts that YOU write and run in your browser (using the GreaseMonkey or TaperMonkey extension) on certain web pages.

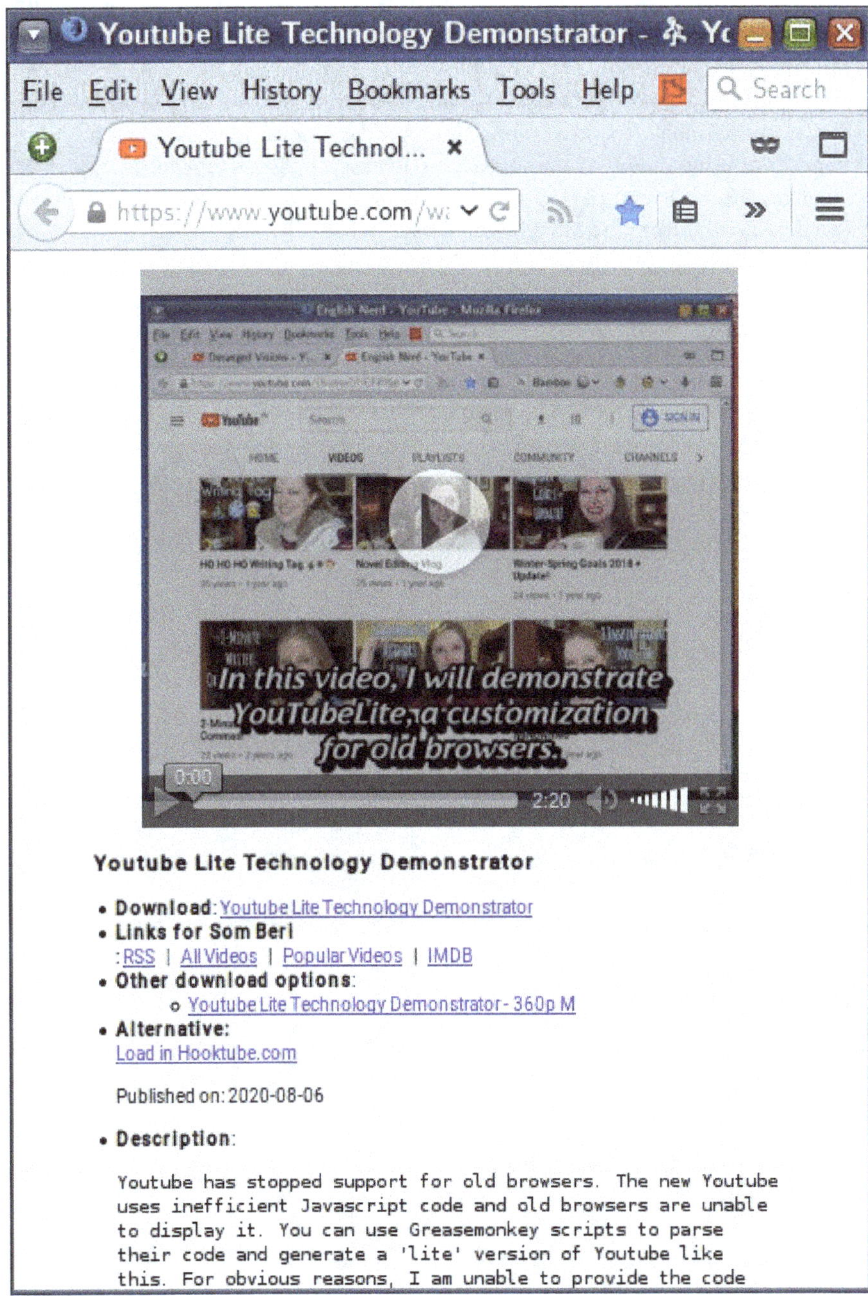

Recently, Youtube took down the command-line video downloader utility Youtube-dl [47]. Online videos are nothing more than a `<video>` HTML tag with an

SRC attribute. If you parse the DOM, you can find the location of the video file in the attribute. After that, you can just download it. This is extremely juvenile stuff. Every 'HTML programmer' knows this. This is not sophisticated enough to call it 'hacking' but Google launched a DMCA attack anyway. They did back off but not before the project was offline for several days.

My Internet connection is so flaky that the Youtube-DL utility never downloads anything fully. I use a decade-old Ubuntu version and its Firefox browser is equally old. Many online video sites stopped support for older browsers. I had to find a way to access online videos. I now have this GreaseMonkey script to download online videos. (The GreaseMonkey add-on is required to run GreaseMonkey scripts. You can download it from the Mozilla Add-Ons microsite.)

On a newer version of the OS (on which this book was created), I have a simpler version of the script that works on any website that hosts videos. You need to disable mediastreaming configuration in the browser for this script to work.

```javascript
// ==UserScript==
// @name        EmbeddedVideoCatcher
// @namespace   com.vsubhash.js.embedded-video-catcher
// @description Adds a link to the video file.
// @include     https://*
// @include     http://*
// @version     2021.02
// @grant       none
// ==/UserScript==

document.addEventListener(
    "readystatechange", loadHandler, false);

function loadHandler() {
  try {
    console.error("EVC: Handled");
    if (document.readyState == "complete") {
      console.error("EVC: loaded");
      addVideoList();
      window.setTimeout(addVideoList, 6*1000);
    } else {
      console.error("EVC: Not loaded");
    }
  } catch (e) { console.error("EVC Error: " + e); }
}

function updateNumberedVideoLink(aoEvent) {
  console.log(
      "EVC: Loaded video event for " + aoEvent.target.src);
  var sTitle = document.title;
```

```javascript
  sTitle = sTitle.replace("- YouTube", "");

  var oLink =
      document.getElementById(
        "jsVidLink" + aoEvent.target.getAttribute("jsVidId"));
  if (oLink) {
    oLink.setAttribute(
        "href", aoEvent.target.getAttribute("src"));
    oLink.innerHTML = sTitle;
  }
}


function addVideoList() {
  var oVideos = document.getElementsByTagName("video");
  if (oVideos.length > 0) {
    console.log("EVC: Number of videos = " + oVideos.length);
    if (document.getElementById("jsVidList")) {
      console.log("EVC: List exists");
    } else {
      var oDlDiv = document.createElement("ul");
      oDlDiv.setAttribute("id", ("jsVidList"));
      oDlDiv.setAttribute("style",
        "position: absolute;
         background-color: rgba(255, 165, 0, 0.8);
         top: 0; display: block; border: 2px dashed firebrick;
         font-size: 0.34cm!important;
         font-family: sans-serif!important;
         line-height: 0.4cm!important;
         margin: 10px 10px 10px 50%;
         padding: 1em; width: 40%; z-index: 3000; ");
      document.getElementsByTagName("body")[0].appendChild(
          oDlDiv);
      console.log("EVC: List added");
    }
    var sTitle = document.title;
    sTitle = sTitle.replace("- YouTube", "");

    for (var i = 0; i < oVideos.length; i++) {
      var oVideoListItem = document.createElement("li");
      if (oVideos[i].src) {
        oVideoListItem.innerHTML =
          "<a id=\"jsVidLink" + i + "\" href=\"" +
          oVideos[i].src + "\">" +  sTitle + "</a>";
      } else {
```

```javascript
        oVideoListItem.innerHTML =
          "<a id=\"jsVidLink" + i +
          "\" href=\"javascript:return(false);\">NA</a>";
      }
      oVideos[i].setAttribute("jsVidId", i);
      oVideos[i].addEventListener(
        "loadeddata", updateNumberedVideoLink, false);
      oDlDiv.appendChild(oVideoListItem);
    }
  } else {
    console.log("EVC: No videos in " + location.href);
  }
}
```

The next script detects RSS feeds in a web page.

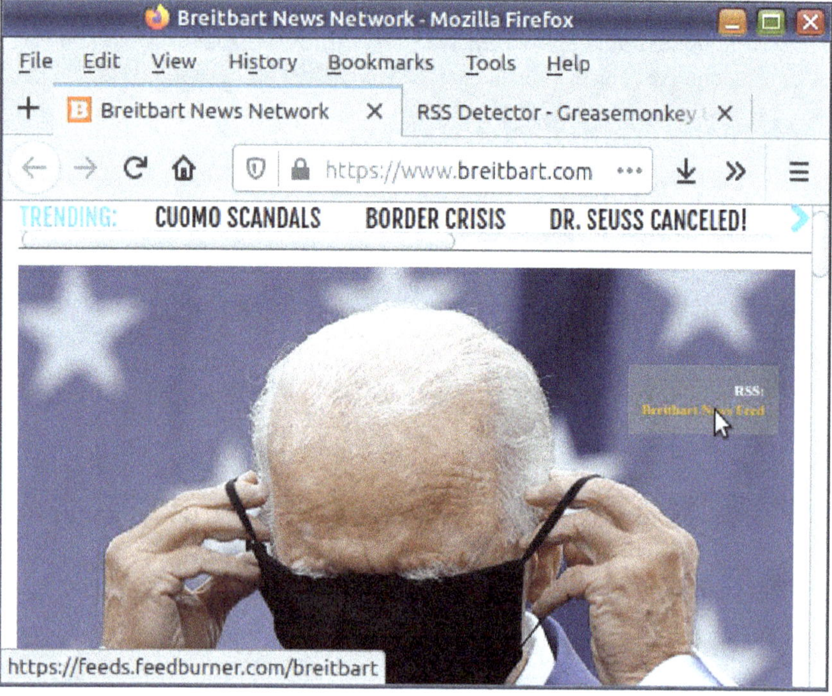


```javascript
// ==UserScript==
// @name       RSS Detector
// @namespace com.vsubhash.js.rss_detector
// @version    1
// @grant      none
// ==/UserScript==

document.addEventListener(
```

```javascript
    "readystatechange",
    function() {
      try {
        if (document.readyState == "complete") {
          //window.setTimeout(findRSS, 2*1000);
          findRSS();
        }
      } catch(e) {
        console.error("RSSD Error: " + e);
      }
    },
    false);


function findRSS() {
  console.log("RSSD: Checking…");

  var oLinks = document.querySelectorAll("link[type*='rss']");
  if (oLinks.length > 0) {
    var oFloater = document.createElement("div");
    oFloater.innerHTML = "RSS:<br />";
    oFloater.style =
        "text-align: right; padding: 1em;
         background-color: lavender;
         color: orange; position: fixed; z-index: 9999;
         font: bold 9px sans-serif; top: 100px; right: 20px; ";
    document.getElementsByTagName("body")[0].insertBefore(
        oFloater,
        document.getElementsByTagName("body")
[0].firstElementChild);
    for (var i = 0; i < oLinks.length; i++) {
      if (oLinks[i].hasAttribute("title") &&
          oLinks[i].hasAttribute("href")) {
        oFloater.innerHTML +=
          "<a href=\"" + oLinks[i].getAttribute("href") + "\">" +
          oLinks[i].getAttribute("title") + "</a><br />";
        console.log(
            "RSSD: Added RSS #" + (i+1) + ": " +
            oLinks[i].getAttribute("title"));
      } else {
        console.log("RSSD: Invalid RSS" + (i+1));
      }
    }
  } else {
```

```javascript
    console.log("RSSD: No RSS found");
  }
}
```

Many websites have unwittingly surrendered their audience to walled gardens like Facebook and Twitter instead of fostering a loyal community using the anonymous RSS technology. It is understandable that companies like Google and Twitter have launched an unofficial war on RSS but it is unforgivable that even Mozilla (makers of the Firefox browser) has joined those enemies of freedom.

When I used to use smartphones, I built an app named **Subhash Browser & RSS Feed Reader**. Yes, I built my own integrated browser and RSS reader app. It also has an integrated read-only file explorer functionality. I hate to use spyware-like apps (Chrome). I also did not like the 'User is stupid' and the grab-everything-as-you-go philosophy of many software programmers and designers. I created Subhash Browser as a privacy- and usability-focused browser loaded to gills with as many features as I could think of. The app stores all data on your phone rather than online. It only takes three app permissions, not everything that other browser apps demand.

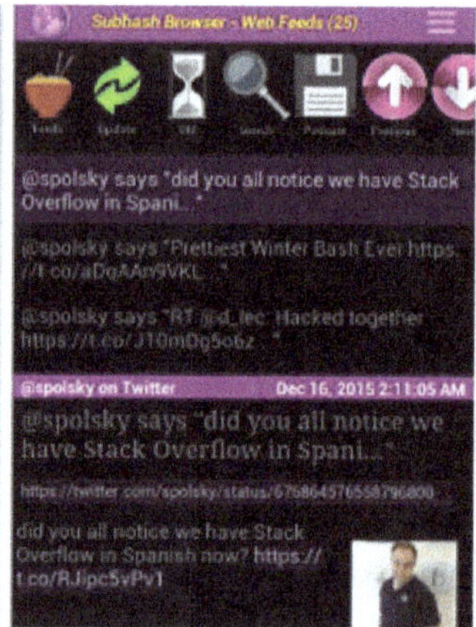
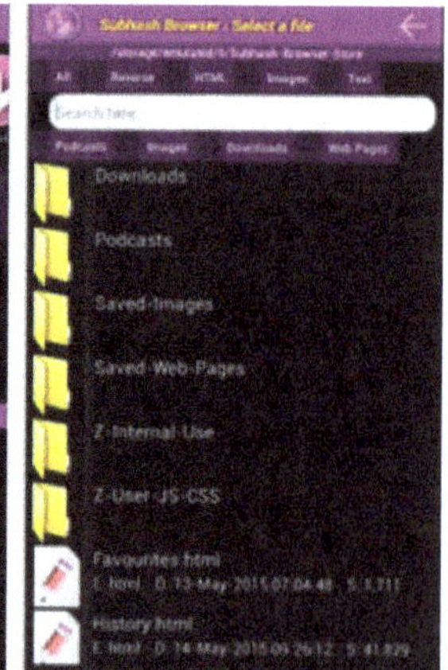

- **Use Stylus:** Similar to user scripts, you can write *user styles* (CSS or stylesheets) and change the look-and-feel of websites in your browser. Place `video { pointer-events: auto!important; }` in a common style. It will enable the built-in right-click menu on most online videos. Stylus is one of many browser extensions that you can use for adding user stylesheets. I have written more on this subject in two articles on CodeProject.com:

  - *User Scripts (JS) and User Styles (CSS)*
  - *"Reader Mode" for Desktop Internet Browsers*

- **Select text inside a link:** In Firefox, you need hold down Ctrl and Alt keys if you need to select text inside a link with your mouse.

- **Disable Javascript:** There was a time when Internet web pages were accessed using text-only console programs. If you feel that modern websites have left you in the cold, then do not worry. Use a Javascript toggle add-on on the toolbar. It also disables ads, social media plugins and even paywalls (low-effort CSS- and Javascript-driven ones). Some websites just do not function without Javascript but in most cases you may do just fine.

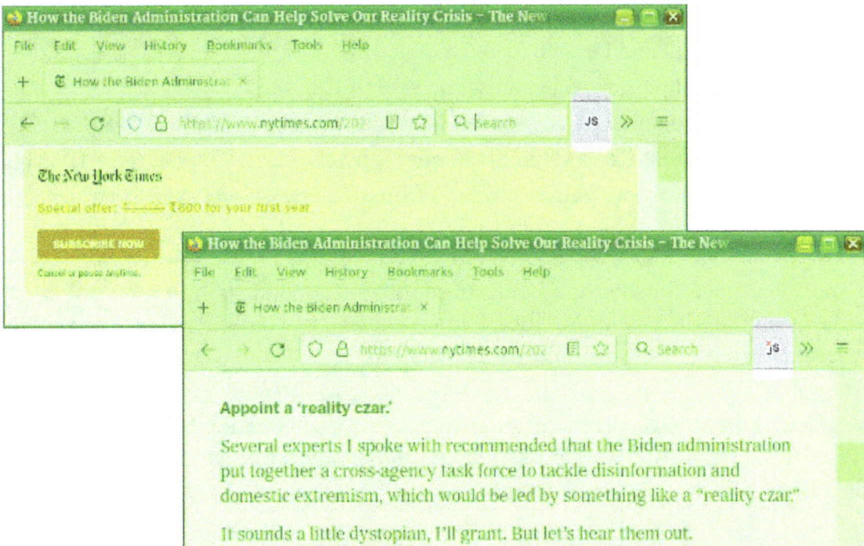

- **Caja tips**:
  - When I moved to the Mate desktop for this book, I found that the file open dialog box in any application did not have the icon button that could be clicked to directly type in the name or path. For some reason, they have dropped it from the dialog. The functionality is still there. You can press **Ctrl+L** to transform the navigation path to an editable text box where you can type the path or filename. You can also press **Ctrl+H** to make hidden files and directories become available in the dialog box.
  - The Ctrl+H keyboard shortcut toggle works in the file manager Caja too. This is because the file open dialog is provided by the Caja to all other applications.
- **More Unicode tricks**:
  - **Strike out without HTML**: In text editors like LibreOffice Writer, strikeout is available as a font style. In HTML, there are S and DEL tags for achieving the same effect. When you are limited to plain text, such as when using MarkDown/CommonMark or using a CMS for data entry, you can use Unicode combining character U+0336 for the same effect. If you type this character (press **CTRL** + **SHIFT** + u, followed by 0336 and then press Enter) after any character, the latter will be struck out as a whole. (You may find it easier to just *copy* this combining character and use the *paste* keyboard shortcut (**CTRL** + V) after every character in the word that needs to be ~~struck out~~.

    There are dozens of these c̈ȯm̈b̈ïn̈ïn̈g characters — from U+300 to U+36F.
  - **Numbered lists**: Some web applications do not allow you to use any kind of formatting. To bypass these restrictions, you can use Unicode codepoints between:
    - U+2460 (①) and U+2473 (⑳)
    - U+24B6 (Ⓐ) and U+24CF (Ⓩ)
    - U+24D0 (ⓐ) and U+24E9 (ⓩ)

- U+2474 ((1)) and U+2487 ((20))
- U+249C ((a)) and U+24B5 ((z))
- U+2488 (1.) and U+249B (20.)

To use bullet points, you can use: ■, ○, ☆,★, •, …

- **Monospaced text**: Use codepoints in ranges from to U+1D670 (A) to U+1D6A3 (z).
- **Cursive letters**: Use codepoints in ranges from to U+1D4D0 ($\mathcal{A}$) to U+1D503 ($\mathfrak{z}$).
- **Bold type**: Use codepoints in ranges from to U+1D5D4 (**A**) to U+1D607 (**z**).

Well, you have finished the book. If you give it a good rating (☆ ☆ ☆ ☆ ☆) or review online, it would be much appreciated. If you have any corrections or suggestions, write to me at Info@VSubhash.Com.

Some of my titles are available for FREE on several ebook stores and library apps. Give them a try. I have written more than two dozen non-fiction books on a wide range of subjects. I have also written ONE fiction title(s)! Check the backlist for more details or visit: www.VSubhash.IN/books.html

---

Useful References

This book is for advanced shell users. If you felt that you could have benefited from a more basic tutorial for the shell and its utilities, then read:

- the *BASH Reference Manual* if you feel strong enough.

  https://www.gnu.org/software/bash/manual/bash.html
- the free tutorial provided by the from the *IEEE* and *The Open Group* at:

  https://pubs.opengroup.org/onlinepubs/9699919799/idx/shell.html

Do not forget...

My book *2020 Fresh Clean Jokes For Everyone*, one of the biggest jokebooks ever, has several chapters for computer and science jokes!

Books By V. Subhash

I invite you to visit my site **WWW.VSUBHASH.IN**, and check out my other books, special discounts, sample PDFs and full ebooks. In 2020, I started publishing books. For two decades before that, I have been publishing feature articles, free ebooks (old editions still available), software (server/desktop/mobile), reviews (books, films, music and travel), funny memes and cartoons. You can follow these adventures on my blog: **http://www.vsubhash.in/blogs/blog/index.html**

My books for children are under the pseudonym **Ólafía L. Óla** (because it has laugh and LOL).

2020 Fresh Clean Jokes For Everyone

This is one of the biggest jokebooks ever written - over 3200 jokes spread over:

- *Part 1 — For Learning* (computer jokes, programming jokes, physics jokes, chemistry jokes, biology jokes, medical jokes, financial jokes, geography jokes, pun jokes and THREE CHAPTERS DEVOTED TO FOREIGN LANGUAGES)
- *Part 2 — For Fun* (bar jokes, blonde jokes, cross-the-road jokes, knock-knock jokes, lightbulb jokes, knock-knock jokes, romantic (breakup) jokes)
- *Part 3 — Only For Intellectuals* (jokes about philosophy, advertising, news and politics)

It has lots of jokes purely for the hedonist consumption of humour, content to improve vocabulary and general knowledge, thought-provoking poems (mostly as financial/political limericks set to the tune of popular nursery rhymes) AND some of the best one-liners EVER written in English. Absolutely no (‿ˣ‿) humour.

• Pages: 292   • Paperback: $10   • Ebook: An older subset with 420 jokes is available for **FREE**

2020 Fresh Clean Jokes For Kids

This 'for kids' subset of the 2020 jokebook has over 2200 jokes. It has all of *Part 1 (For Learning)* and some non-political jokes from *Part 2 (For Fun)* & *Part 3 (Only For Intellectuals)*. Joke types include computer jokes, programming jokes, cross-the-road jokes, physics jokes, chemistry jokes, biology jokes, medical jokes, financial jokes, geography jokes, knock-knock jokes, breakup jokes...). Special chapters include *Elephant & Ant Jokes*, *Off-The-Wall Philosophers*, *Useful French Phrases*, *Useful Latin Phrases*, *Other Useful Foreign Phrases*, *Jokes You Love To Hate*, *Jokes In Advertising*, and *Fancy Creature Jokes*. No political or controversial jokes. Absolutely no (‿ˣ‿) humour.

• Pages: 166   • Paperback: ₹550 or $7.70   • Ebook: Will never be published

Ólafía L. Óla's Favourite Traditional Nursery Rhymes (Illustrated)

The political correctness pandemic has caused many nursery rhymes to be rewritten or eliminated altogether. This illustrated children's book has **50 popular English nursery rhymes in their traditional form**. The selected rhymes have stood the test of time and this **large-print paperback with edge-to-edge colour** makes it easy for kids to read them.

• Pages: 44 (39 with real content)   • Colour
Paperback: $9 • Ebook: $2

Animalia Humorosum

This is an illustrated children's storybook based on Aesop's Fables. The stories have been made more believable by changing the ending with a humorous twist. **The book is a large-print paperback with edge-to-edge colour.**

• Pages: 30 (26 with real content)   • Colour Paperback: $9   • Ebook (for parental review): ₹70 or $2 or FREE

World of Word Ladders

Word ladders are a wonderful pastime. These puzzles are neither tough nor easy. They have the right balance between exercising the brain and having fun. Word ladders can challenge a kid's thinking ability, spelling skills and vocabulary. For an adult, word ladders are pure fun. A word ladder has a diagram of a ladder with a word on both the first and last rungs. You need to change only one letter in the blank middle rungs so that the first word is transformed into the last word. Next to each word ladder is its solution. The solution is obscured to protect the challenge. Here are some examples:

* **C-A-T** » *C-O-T* » *C-O-G* » **D-O-G**
* **L-A-S-T** » *L-O-S-T* » *L-O-S-E* » *H-O-S-E* » **H-O-P-E**

• Puzzles: 100 • Paperback: $6 (per volume)

Vastu Shastra Explained

This is a plain-English Vástu Śastra building-architecture guide for those who wish to draw their own Vastu-compliant house plans. The book does not upsell Vaastu as a panacea for all ills nor does it portray Vastu as the Indian Feng Shui. Instead, it presents Vastu as a collection of time-tested best-practices in Indian building architecture.

This book is based on the *Vastu Shastra* given in *Matsya Purana*. A PDF containing the original English translation is available for free on my website.

• Pages: 38 (31 with real content)   • Colour Paperback: $7.77   • Ebook: ₹100 or $6

Learn To Ride A Motorcycle In Five Minutes

Yes, you can! For most of my life, I did not know how to ride a motorbike. But, when I had to do, it took me only five minutes. On my first ride on my first bike, I travelled nearly 100 kilometres, across two cities and one national highway. Acquiring the skill takes less than five minutes and honing it will require a few weeks.

• Pages: 40 (30 with real content)
• Paperback: $7.70   • Ebook: ₹100 or $6

How To Invest In Stocks, 2nd Edition

The first edition book was written in 2003 for the Indian stockmarket. It was popular around the world because it was a plain-English guide to investing in the stockmarket. The 2020 completely revised second edition maintains the original premise but has a global focus, updated information and new chapters. **It has some useful 'extra' information that you will not find in any investment book and no business school will teach you.** Mere book knowledge about stockmarkets will not help you understand the markets. Markets are influenced by news and information (there is a difference).

• Pages: 94   • Paperback: $9.90   • Ebook: ₹100 or $3

Email Newsletter Strategies For Profit

An organically grown mailing list is an invaluable resource for your business. It is your own social network. You need to nurture it like a baby. This book not only explains how to create user-friendly email newsletters but also helps you improve email deliverability, organically grow your mailing list, implement industry-standard best-practices and apply practical troubleshooting tips and tricks.

• Pages: 40 (33 with real content)   • Paperback: $7.70   • Ebook: ₹100 or $3

How To Cure Common Cold

Non-allergic rhinitis or common cold is an ailment that usually resolves on its own. It can be very disruptive and make you feel miserable. *How To Cure Common Cold* **describes several palliative measures** (not curative options) that can be used to treat the symptoms while the body fights off the infection. Because this is a thin topic, **bonus content** on natural weight-loss techniques, an easy-to-cook vegetarian food recipe, dental care tips, skincare tips, and some family-planning advice are included in this book. **DISCLAIMER**: The author is not a medical professional. Despite seeking medical treatment for common cold, his deviated nasal septum made the episodes very difficult to go through. Over several years, he tried and tested several palliative measures to treat the symptoms. In this book, he describes what measures might work for young healthy individuals like him. These recommendations are not intended for kids, adolescents, convalescents, seniors or in people where the cold symptoms are part of a larger ailment.**This book is not sponsored by any drug firm or commercial entity.**

• Pages: 31 (8 with real content)   • Paperback: $4.99   • Ebook: ₹99 or $1 or `FREE`

The Devil's Dictionary

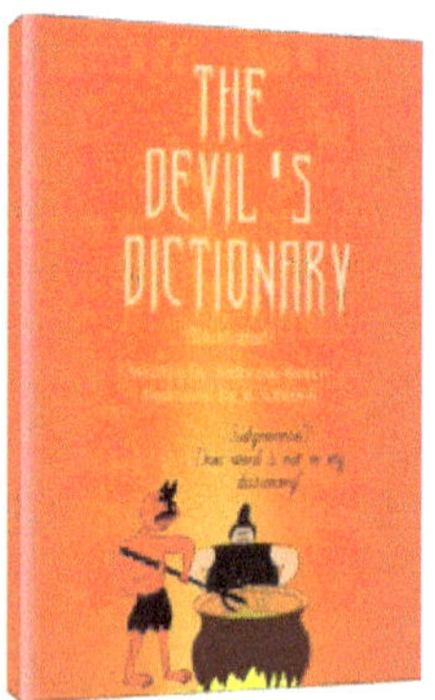

The Devil's Dictionary by Ambrose Bierce from 1911 is a great repository of brutally frank and unusually cynical descriptions for popular words and phrases in English. In my 2020 remake, the original text has been illustrated with contemporary caricatures (of Alexandria Ocasio Cortez, Bill Gates, Don Lemon, Elon Musk, Joe Biden...). It has the **neat easy-on-the-eye look of any new dictionary (modern fonts, two-column pages, starting/ending words on every page)**. If you consider yourself as a woke, liberal, Leftie, Progressive, Socialist, Communist, Feminist... then this book is not for you. This book by Bierce is a product of its time and may not match your unrealistic expectations. Maybe, you could gift it to your (fr)enemies. They might like it.

• Pages: 160   • Paperback: $9   • Ebook: ₹100 or $2

Quick Start Guide to FFmpeg

FFmpeg is THE BEST software to easily create, edit, enhance and convert audio and video files. It is a FREE and open-source command-utility available **for Linux, Mac and Windows**. And, *Quick Start Guide to FFmpeg* is THE BEST book for an extensive FFmpeg tutorial, hack collection and quick reference. It is richly illustrated with color screenshots, code examples and tables to help you work with audio, video, images, animations, fonts,

subtitles and metadata like a PRO. NOTE: In 2023, the old self-published book *FFmpeg Quick Hacks* was withdrawn.

• Pages: 280   • Colour Paperback: $44.99   • PDF Ebook: $29.99 (from Apress/SpringerNature)

CommonMark Ready Reference

MarkDown is an easy human-readable text format that can serve as the common base for exporting to multiple document formats such as HTML, ODF, DOC/DOCX, PDF and ebook (EPUB, MOBI…). It is a great tool for authors, technical writers and content developers to create books, manuals, web pages and other rich-text content. CommonMark is a new well-formed standard for the old MarkDown spec. **CommonMark was one of the reasons I was able to write and design 21 books in one year.** Incidentally, this is the first-ever book on CommonMark. You will be buying a piece of history! The paperback's covers are designed like a quick reference card.

• Pages: 56 (39 with real content, 6 with bonus content)   • Paperback: $7   • Ebook: **FREE** or ₹70 or $1

Linux Command-Line Tips & Tricks

This is a tips-and-tricks collection for Linux command-line warriors. It is also at an advanced level. It assumes that you already know how to use the terminal and are adept at shell programming. It does not teach you the basics or try to be a comprehensive reference. It trusts your intuition and focuses on things you are most likely to forget. Because of its ancient history, BASH scripting has some odd programming constructs that are difficult to memorize. This book tries to provide a ready-reference for such archaic but crucial details. It pays special attention to coding mistakes or unusual circumstances in which your script or command will fail. The paperback has screenshots and syntax-highlighted code examples, all in full-colour.

• Pages: 100   • Colour Paperback: $9.99   • Ebook: ₹200 or $5

PC Hardware Explained

You can build a PC in 30 minutes with just a screwdriver. Knowing which computer components will work together is not so easy. This full-colour paperback will explain computer hardware using **simple terms, illustrations, photographs and tables**. Before **buying a new laptop from the store** or **assembling a new desktop from parts**, get this book. You will be able to read the technical specifications of a PC and understand what it can and cannot do. The mumbo-jumbo accompanying the sales pitch of a new computer will not be so alien.

• Pages: 30 (22 with real content)   • Colour paperback: $7   • Ebook: ₹100 or $3

Cool Electronic Projects

If you are learning electronics or thinking of it as a future hobby, this FULL-COLOUR book has some fun projects to begin with. They will not waste your time or money, will be extremely useful (particularly in emergencies) and are quite easy to make. Just one of these projects uses AC (alternating current). The rest work on DC (direct current) and are safe for kids (if you think soldering is safe). These projects are good for the environment too, as they reuse electronic parts that would have been discarded. If you are a survivalist, then you will be happy that all the projects will run off-the-grid, as they can consume renewable energy. For the tinkerer, there are projects that add MORE POWER than what the manufacturer had provided. For the parent of lazy children, there are annoying alarms that can wake up the dead.

• Pages: 40 (33 with real content)   • Paperback: $9.90   • Ebook: ₹100 or $3

How To Install Solar

This is a heavily illustrated guidebook for **INDIAN** solar power enthusiasts, DIY hacks, home-owners and electricians about solar panels, batteries, inverters, charge controllers, installation procedures and costs. It starts with a simple introduction to home electrical systems, proceeds on to describe various aspects of solar power and options available for home owners, and then provides step-by-step instructions for installing a low-cost DC-only solar charge controller system for ₹6000 and a solar inverter system providing AC power backup for ₹30,000. Also included is an extensive FAQs section based on questions and reviews published by solar power users online.

• Pages: 76   • Colour paperback: $7.70   • Ebook: ₹100 or $3

Unlikely Stories

This is an anthology of horror and comedy stories — an exorcism, an alien encounter, a haunted lift, a seance, a shapeshifter, a werewolf, a talking bird, an evil twin, an alien invasion and a distressed young alpaca — all weaved into a witty love yarn. The author originally intended to write a non-fiction book based on real-life incidents. He was however **forced by several governments** to name this book as 'Unlikely Stories' and release it only as a fiction title. The stories have turned out to be **supernatural, paranormal and sci-fi fantasies with ample doses of action, horror and humour**. The entire book is in first person and everything happens very fast. There is never a dull moment.

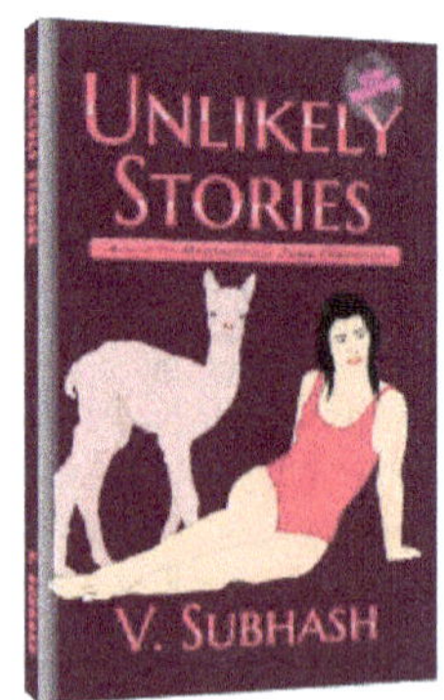

First edition stories

- **The trip**: The lead is invited by his friend to a resort where he meets the first heroine. He nicknames her *Vampira*.

- **The swim**: The lead decides that Vampira is the soul mate he has been waiting all his life. He tells several stories to entertain his friend's kids and also impress Vampira.
- **The exorcist**: The second lead is an Indian crook who escapes to the West to start a new life. He attempts to go legit but finds competition from a professional medium operating under the trade name of *Mademoiselle Zuma*. She is dangerous because she is a mind-reader.
- **Alien encounter**: After the successful exorcism, this lead is asked to help a teenager who has been repeatedly 'abducted' by an alien.
- **The lift**: A recently deceased security guard haunts a lift where he had died and seeks revenge.
- **Femme fatale**: The second lead has a showdown with a female animal spirit.
- **The seance**: A young woman in the city is troubled by nightmares involving a hooded skeleton. A newly married nurse blanks out every night. She is also troubled by bizarre nightmares. Mademoiselle Zuma solves both cases.
- **The haunting**: An old mansion is haunted by a presence. Every new buyer and his family gets driven to such desperation that they eventually sell. The second lead investigates and almost gets killed.
- **Family planning**: The first lead and Vampira plan their life together. In the first ending, they get married. In the second ending (written by the lead after their first night), **Stone Age Man (SAM)** and **Stone Age Woman (SAW)** discover the mystery of life. (This is an over-the-top parody of the **controversy about *MEN WRITING WOMEN***.) Other than some intimate events implied in comic fashion in this story, there is no physical contact between the sexes in the entire book. Not even a kiss. The book is clean throughout. No swear words. No corny mushy dialogue. No degeneracy. No weirdness. Just no low-hanging fruit.

New stories in second edition
(*Mademoiselle Zuma Chronicles*)

- **Shadows in the night**: A young woman is troubled by a ghostly intruder at night.
- **Zuma vs. Cutie**: Zuma finds competition from an unlikely friend.
- **The evil twin**: A rich heiress is driven to desperation by a deceased twin who wants her to die as well.
- **Alien chicks are nothing but trouble**: A meteorite crashes down in the Atlantic. The site becomes an alien platform for launching attacks on English-speaking countries. No other countries are attacked. The world's sole superpower collapses after a few days. That is not strangest thing about the invasion. The invaders' primary objective is not humans but cows. This is no run-of-the-mill alien-invasion story. Uniquely, it provides a fascinating and realistic economic model for a successful alien invasion of Earth.
- **Please do not smile at our alpaca**: Zuma and her husband restart a farm devastated by the aliens. Things go well until her husband picks a fight with a South American.

NOTE: The second edition has several stories written from the perspective of Zuma.

• Second-edition colour paperback (122 pages, 15 stories): $9.99   • Second-edition grayscale paperback: $9   • Second-edition ebook: ₹200 or $3

• First-edition grayscale paperback (144 pages, 10 stories): $7.77   • First-edition ebook: FREE or ₹100 or $1.99

About the author

You will never find another guy with so many talents as this one! V. Subhash is an invisible Indian writer, programmer, cartoonist and humourist. He grew up in Chennai but is now settled in his native Kerala. In 2020, he published one of the biggest jokebooks of all time — *2020 Fresh Clean Jokes For Everyone* . Subhash was inspired to write it after years of listening to vintage American radio shows such as *Fibber & Molly* and *Duffy's Tavern* . In the same year, he followed up with a how-to book on the multimedia software FFmpeg and a 400-page volume of 149 political cartoons. How did he do that? Subhash pursues numerous hobbies and interests that inevitably became the subject of his books — like *Cool Electronic Projects* , *How To Invest In Stocks* and *How To Install Solar* . He used to have pet tortoises but they died in a parking accident. Everyone was  crushed. For two decades before 2020, Subhash used his personal website **www.VSUBHASH.in** as the main outlet for his writing while also accumulating a lot of unpublished material. By 2022, he had exhausted all that he could publish. Meanwhile, his probe into 'aliens' had revealed that they are just ordinary employees/contractors of US military and space agencies. They begged him not to write anything so he published his findings in his debut fiction title named *Unlikely Stories* . The stories turned out to be supernatural/paranormal/sci-fi fantasies with ample doses of action, horror and humour. In 2023, Apress (SpringerNature) published his rewritten and updated FFmpeg book as *Quick Start Guide To FFmpeg* .